# Savoring
### the Sacred,
## the Real, and the True

*Contemplative Responses to Scripture*
Matthew – John

Julia S. Ledford

# Endorsements

You will enjoy this experience! This is not a book to read; rather, it is a book to pray. It will invoke a deeper, ongoing conversation with God. As you pray, you will reflect and rejoice on insights gained from the Spirit. Your prayers will focus on heart-searching contemplation. You will discover that God has heard, and that God cares.

This is a book of faith "that the New Testament is a true record of a world-changing, life-altering, eternity-sealing, ongoing act of God." This is a new way of reading and experiencing the Bible! You are invited to: Read, Pray, Think, Reflect, and Respond.

Author Julia Ledford has experienced the journey. She has recorded in this book an approach to Bible study and meditation that will help readers escape the wilderness and proceed toward the Promised Land!

Bruce P. Powers
Langston Professor of Christian Education
Campbell University Divinity School
Buies Creek, North Carolina

Through the slow and prayerful reading of the gospels, this book of prayers offers rhythm and a structure to reading the gospels and reconnects you with God — God in the holy scriptures, God within you, and God within the world and all creation. In my own life, I found such a reading to be formative, refreshing and yet personally challenging as I engaged scripture and God in new ways.

Deedra Rich
Instructor, Spirituality Program, Columbia Theological Seminary

Christ-followers who long for transformative experiences with God will find this prayer book to be a faithful partner in the journey. Not only did this book of prayers call me to set aside time to engage my spirit with the gospel passages, but Julia's prayers often sent me back to the same Scripture passage eagerly focusing on what I overlooked that she so eloquently and thoughtfully captured in her authentic conversation with the Holy One.

Dr. Clella Lee
Leadership Consultant, Christian Women's Leadership Center

If used as she intends, Julia Ledford's book of prayers will apply the brakes to your runaway train of life and give you a second breath before you must careen around the next curve. *Savoring the Sacred, the Real and the True: Contemplative Responses to Scripture* is such a brake lever.

*Savoring the Sacred* is not a Bible study. Julia is not going line by line, parsing the Greek derivatives. More than an exposition of word and phrases, she captures the spirit of each selected passage, nourishes it with insight and releases it to bless your soul.

Filled with humility and transparency, Julia admonishes us that "this is not a book to read; rather it is a book to pray." There are bookshelves and libraries filled with books on prayer, about prayer, how to pray, of prayers and Julia humbly acknowledges that the last thing she wanted to produce was another placeholder on someone's shelf. If you get this book and leave it on the shelf, you will be missing both a blessing and an opportunity for growth.

She reminded me that it is a frightening, humbling and awesome privilege to approach the living God. We are pots clinging precariously to a wobbly table top and a single breath by a displeased potter could shatter us on the floor. Yet we approach God casually and act presumptively.

Julia's prayers are confessional, transparent, insightful, yearning, soulful. She encourages you not to "pray HER prayers" but to use them as a guide. Use her words if you will and if you must, but her greater joy will be when you see her words only as rocks that pave the road to your own prayers. You cannot approach the living God as someone else or on the back of another, or on the prayers or deeds of someone else. Ultimately, you come to God as an individual and Julia's prayerful insights into the passages she has chosen will help you abrade your protective scales and step outside of your insulation to show God willingly what He can already see without your permission: your bleeding, tearful soul, unshackled, free at last, ready to grow out of and away from our Christian cultural expectations into the freedom fields of true communion with God.

She confesses, from Matthew 8:21-34, that her "fear is real and remains." She admits she has "preferred to socialize with the attractive and affluent when you would draw aside to dine with the unattractive, unclean and even despised." From Luke 17:20-37 she confesses a misguided clamoring for success and now, "I stand before your unpredictable and uncontrollable power and am dismayed. I am unworthy and overwhelmed by the jeopardy in which I have lived."

The jeopardy in which I have lived. Julia's book of prayers will help you step out of the jeopardy of presumption upon God and into the security and blessing of relationship.

Norman Jameson
Writer, Advancement Consultant
WordsAndDeeds.me

# Contents

# Introduction

To all those who choose to at least look over this book, thank you! I hope you will decide to read it prayerfully. I encourage you to do more than read it, for it is a book of prayer. Therefore, my real desire is that you will pray with me. These prayers arose in response to scripture as I read through the Gospels. So, actually, this is not a book to read; rather it is a book to pray. To a large extent, it is a book that is intended to invoke a deeper, ongoing conversation with God.

So, let's talk about what this book is not! This is not intended to be a typical book *of* prayers nor a book *about* prayer. It is not an intellectual treatise or doctrinal commentary, though personal commentary is naturally woven into the prayers. The prayers are meant to reflect a conversation with God, with musings expressed as much as petitions. Overall, it is a believing response, full of trust, reverence, and even questions for the One True God, whose yearning for us underlies all of life, especially the gospel of Jesus Christ.

Through these prayers, I hope to foster a dialogue between the Word of God, the reader — and the world. These prayers emerged in response to devotional, reflective, repeated readings of each passage in the ancient *Lectio Divina* style. Rather than reading a passage three to four times at one sitting as in *Lectio Divina*, each passage was read daily for three to four days until a prayer of response emerged to be articulated. If I were to begin all over again, each prayer would be different — as I would be reading, meditating, and responding within a different context of my life. So the reader may find that some prayers "fit" and some do not. I encourage each person to pray their own prayers more than mine, but I hope that my prayers will inspire them to dig even deeper into scripture for a more meaningful communion with God.

Above all, this is a book of faith expressing that the New Testament is a true record of the world-changing, life-altering, eternity-sealing, ongoing act of God. The overall interpretation is viewed through the lens of God's magnificent love, which triumphs over Judgment and extends Grace, Mercy, and Hope to every person who seeks God with an open, honest heart.

It is my prayer that each person who reads (and prays) this book will encounter the truth of God's love in a fresh way, and be encouraged to follow His Son Jesus down the path of life with increasing and unwavering fidelity. My hope is that it will open a fresh and meaningful perspective on the pathway into all the rich treasures of God's Word in the Gospels.

I have used the Revised Standard Version (RSV) primarily because that is in my heart language — the version that my heart has come to know with intimacy and familiarity over many years. However, I would encourage readers to engage with these texts using a translation that speaks to each person's own soul and that releases the truth within God's loving revelation. For some passages, I also followed the New International Version (NIV) or King James Version (KJV) when the translation illuminated the passage with fresh insight for me. References quoted from each focal passage are identified by quotation marks without text citations, but other quoted passages are cited in the endnotes.

Overall, I have sought to pray and write with a sense of community, for I have learned that we are never fully with God until we accept our place among all the others loved by God. So, plural pronouns are used often. However, there are times when I have chosen to use singular personal pronouns to assist the reader in personalizing the prayers.

I know that we must recognize our joint commonality before God, and that no one is an island unto himself — or God. He created and redeemed us all for union together with Him. I am aware that, while these prayers are personally mine, they may also serve as a reflection of the needs and experiential faith of each one of us who are a part of the Christian community. We were all created for union with God and Jesus' last prayer was for all who believe in Him to be One in the union that He has with God the Father (John 17).

So, when we pray, we can never truly pray alone. Jesus' model prayer begins "Our" Father because we never pray in isolation. However, that being said, sometimes the heart cries out in the singular. Sometimes we feel very alone, isolated by our misdeeds and the misdeeds of others, or by our own misplaced affections and desires. My overarching intent has been to make these prayers the human outpourings of "ordinary" believers, shaped in the personal conversational ways that we often pray when we pray from the heart. In those times, feel free to pray any of these prayers in the first person. Cry out as "I" in need of God's grace. Bow before the Holy God, pleading, "Have mercy upon *me*."

# Appreciation

I must first of all express my gratitude to my mother, who taught me to pray on my knees beside her, where I heard the words of "forgiveness" and "protection" for the first time, and recognized them as great treasures to be sought from the Lord our God. In my child's imagination, I envisioned protection as a gleaming circle of silver, and forgiveness as a bright circle of gold. I have sought and treasured them all of my life as God's cherished, imperishable gifts.

I also have deep appreciation for my husband, who has encouraged my growth in faith and ministry. Neither of us ever dreamed that I would be called into formal ministry. We were both born in the 1940s and grew up in the era of the 1950s and '60s. Within the culture of that day, women worked, for the most part, at home or in one of three professions: teacher, nurse, or secretary. I chose the latter until I found that my soul was drying up for lack of a sense of fulfillment. Gradually, I grew to understand a call into ministry, which unfolded over a period of thirty years and into various roles.

In opportunities for worship leadership, it felt natural to me to seek the guidance of the Holy Spirit in preparation — including the writing of prayers for congregational worship. Over a period of fifteen years, I was encouraged by a surprising number of people of all ages to publish a book of my prayers, but was reluctant to add yet another book to the shelves. My own shelves bulged with such books and that is a minor treasury of the world's great writings on prayer. It seemed preposterous for me to expect to write a collection of prayers that might find a place among them. Whether this ends up in such a position, or only in the hands of a few friends, I am grateful to friends at Hayes Barton Baptist Church and beyond who urged me to publish.

I am grateful to the universal church at large for the heritage of faith and spiritual practice that was handed on to me, and I hope to participate in that ongoing dissemination of the gospel through this writing. My heritage began in the small-town, grassroots evangelical belief systems of denominations rooted in revivalist culture. As I moved into formal ministry, I was blessed with exposure to other traditions and theological viewpoints. While I remain a simple believer of the basic gospel handed on to me, I appreciate the freedom and enrichment that I found in the wider theological reflections and historical practices of Christian tradition. The writings of many ancient and current Christian thinkers have enriched my faith and shaped my understanding, providing a rich backdrop for my prayerful reflections.

I am happy also to have had the support of professors and colleagues at Campbell University and Divinity School, who helped me believe in my place in professional ministry. In the 1980s, I was affirmed in my calling to ministry while studying at Southeastern Baptist Theological Seminary. I have also been encouraged by connections with fellow pilgrims and faculty in the Spiritual Formation certification program of Columbia Theological Seminary. Altogether and individually, many persons have helped me to believe that there is an ear for my written prayers. To them, I am deeply appreciative.

Above all, I have been blessed to know Jesus as Lord and Savior since I was seven years old, and I offer utmost praise to God for leading me to Jesus so that He could bring me to God! What a wonderful arrangement of Grace for us all! In other words, I gladly proclaim that all of my life is a gift from God and this latest adventure could not have happened without His loving hand guiding all along the way.

# *Foreword*

In writing these prayers, I have written primarily for those who are learning to seek God in quietness. God commanded Moses to take off his shoes, because he was on Holy Ground. When we have our shoes on, we are ready for action, so God signified that we would find Him when we stopped our everyday endeavors for focused intervals with Him. This book is for those who are ready to recognize and reverently enter the holy setting into which we place ourselves when we read and pray in response to scripture. The reader may find it helps them focus if they literally take off their shoes as a physical act of recognition that we enter God's presence when we read scripture and pray.

We remember that God said to the Psalmist, "Be still and know that I am God" (Psalm 46:10). Elijah too learned that lesson (1 Kings 19:12). He had sought God as we often do — in bold expressions of power and might. He was surprised to hear God's voice only when he quit that search and stood still in quiet expectancy and intense listening — and was able to finally hear a still, small voice. Moses learned to turn aside and stand in the holy place where God would commune with him (Exodus 3:2). Jesus engaged in a balance of prayer, solitude, and community, slipping off into the hillsides for time alone with His Father (Matthew 14:23). The biblical model is clear. We need to spend time alone, still and quiet, with God.

In Psalm 23, we are shown images of God as our Good Shepherd, leading us to lie down in green pastures and rest beside still waters, nurtured and satisfied. I have found that experience is possible when I take time, long periods of time, to sit still with God and His Word in living and loving communion. Jesus said to enter our inner room (closet) to meet God who sees us in secret, and I have come to understand the deeper invitation is to enter the realm of our soul, where no one else ever really knows us but God. We are surprised to find God there, in our hidden inner soul, yet Jesus also said, "The Kingdom of God is within You" (Luke 17:21). Taken together, these passages offer an invitation to find God within rather than far away, close rather than distant, loving and welcoming rather than blaming and excluding.

The prayers are based on scripture, so just as some passages are long and others are brief, some prayers are long and others are relatively brief. Feel free to read in segments if your time allotment requires brevity, but I encourage you to stretch your time frame by re-arranging your daily activities to open a longer window of time for meeting with the God who has your back for time and eternity.

I would encourage you to take this opportunity to establish a new way of reading scripture, if you are not already engaging in this practice. *Lectio Divina* is an ancient process of reading and reflecting that enhances our capacity to discern the truth of scripture that the Spirit seeks to speak into our hearts and to work into our lives.

While I recognize that some of you may not feel you can follow my preferred way of engaging with this book, I recommend that you at least try to read in the manner outlined below:

I.    Remind yourself that you come to a place to meet God when you come to His divinely inspired Word in scripture.

II.    Read the focal passage through once, slowly and prayerfully, for content.

III.    Slowly read the passage a second time, reflecting on the words, phrases, characters, and actions that most claim your attention.

IV.    Read again slowly and pray in response to what the Spirit is impressing on your mind and heart.

V.    Sit silently for at least five minutes, allowing no conscious thoughts to dominate. Attempt to fulfill God's yearning for you to "Be still and know that I am God" (Psalm 46:10). Listen with your soul.

VI.    The next step is to read and personalize the prayer I have written for the focal passage you have encountered.

VII.    Reflect and rejoice on insights gained from the Spirit. Record new understandings and fresh revelations in a journal and/or write your own prayer of response! Who knows, maybe you, too, will publish a book of prayers! I would love to know that my simple book had inspired that!

# *Praying Through Matthew*

## Matthew 1

*Read carefully and prayerfully as suggested in the Foreword.* Reflect on the truth that speaks most clearly to you. Pray your own prayer in response to the Word of the Spirit to you. Offer the following prayer if it helps you express your thoughts to the Lord.

### Prayer of Response

This is where it all begins — the stories in which our Christian faith is rooted — stories of wonder, obedience, dreams, prophesies, Spirit. From our "enlightened" cultural perspective, many dismiss what this story purports. Yet here we hear the message that will come to us often in the New Testament, the message we long to trust: "Do not be afraid."

Why do we fear, Lord? Why do we still get entangled in the restrictions and anxieties of the Law? Why do we still allow cultural dogma to define our lives? Why does public disgrace terrorize us so? I am probably only beginning to understand that our fears are rooted in our abiding sense of being unloved and unworthy before You, Our Creator. For many, perhaps for most, there is an ingrained understanding of self due to unloving experiences in life. Help us to trust in our belovedness before You, Our Father in heaven who loves us like a mother. Help us "see" You as You lift up Your countenance and smile lovingly toward us.

Here we have the marvelous account of how You began to work in our world to release us from the bondage that religious law had created, along with its soul-crushing sense of unworthiness. Under the Law, we stand quaking before a relentless judge, who only loves us when we repent and live with clean hands and a pure heart ever after. In the Gospels, a loving Father comes to us before we are worthy and offers to wrap us in unquenchable love, like the babe wrapped in swaddling clothes, and continues to love us with undefeatable love, even as we muddle along.

So, this is a welcome story of an unlikely scenario — the conception and birth of a baby, a son, to a humble couple, albeit with important genealogical ties to the story of God from Adam until Jesus. There was no recognized aristocracy. Certainly there was no breathless expectation that the Messiah would come to them, especially to a woman pregnant before her wedding consummation. Though many Jewish families hoped to bring forth God's Messiah, it's unlikely that anyone would have chosen Joseph and Mary for that role. Lord, few would choose me either. I have nothing that the world, even the religious world, would deem very worthy. I'm too ordinary.

Therein lies the beauty of Your coming to ordinary folks in an ordinary place and going about an ordinary life — in extra-ordinary ways. The marvel of the story is summed up in one beautiful name: "Immanuel." What a glorious message in the name: "God with us." Immanuel — Jesus — a babe destined to save his people from their sins. What? His people, devoted to the Law, needed to be saved from their sins? People scrupulously keeping to what they believed to be God's very prescription for them as his people — they needed to be saved from their sins? Then surely I need to.

Surely we all need to be saved from our sins. The good news is truly good news: the message that we are loved. In this story, we are touched by compassion as it is fleshed out in Joseph — a man who really loved both God and Mary, and sought only to do what was loving for both of those commitments. In him, we begin to see God's love unfold to us — a tender, compassionate love.

O God who is with us, I open to Your love and thank You for it. Amen.

# Matthew 2

*Read carefully and prayerfully.* Reflect on the truth that speaks most clearly to you. Pray your own prayer in response to the Word of the Spirit to you. Offer the following prayer if it helps you express your thoughts to the Lord.

## Prayer of Response

This is typical, Lord. It could just as easily have happened in our day. A star rose and only a few took note. Why? Was the King too busy to gaze at the night sky? Did the natural world no longer inspire wonder? Had the people long since forgotten the words of the prophet, or had they ceased to pay attention or to believe that a ruler would come to shepherd God's people? Were the King and religious rulers too caught up in their sense of power and authority to long for a ruler over them? Were they too satisfied with their own level of affluence and comfort to care that God's people lacked a shepherd and were crying out — from their hovels, their byways, hillsides and valleys — for God's care and guidance as their Good Shepherd? Where do we find ourselves in this account? Where am I?

Thank You, O God, that You hear the humble prayers of dismissed people. Thank You that dreams still may convey Your messages and that You still send messengers. Help us listen. Thank You that You still speak to those whose ears are attentive and minds are open, those with hearts longing and souls welcoming. How sad that the people of that day, and ours, so seldom listen. Forgive me for my own deafness.

How disheartening and terrifying to know that people will scheme, plot, and carry out devious plans, even murderous plans to wipe out the innocent — even precious little children — in order to protect their status, wealth, or agendas. Yet we hear of it in the news or see it on our television and computer screens every day, sometimes even more close at hand. The frightening part is that so little is done about it. We shake our heads and turn away, back to our busy lives. Few take the time to hold a vigil. Around the world, day and night, mothers cry out for their children who are no more. Children cry out for their fathers and mothers who are no more. Loud cries of weeping and mourning arise from horrendous losses that can never be comforted. And it seethes in the collective consciousness of the world, weighing us down, deadening our souls with a sense of hopelessness and rage-driven retaliation.

Thank You for this message that You came into a world just like ours and brought hope. Lord, come again, afresh and anew. No, wait, that isn't the right prayer, is it? Lord, here am I, send me to speak what needs to be spoken, and to live out what needs to be expressed in action. Help me step out of my busyness and make time to care for those who are dismissed and misled, victimized and terrorized. Help Your people everywhere to flesh out the gospel in ways that raise hope throughout the world — one simple act of kindness at a time, as well as monumental endeavors of courage. It is our only hope. The Messiah has come. The message has been declared. We are now the messengers.

In the name of the One from Bethlehem, ruler and shepherd of God's people, Amen.

# Matthew 3

*Read carefully and prayerfully.* Reflect on the truth that speaks most clearly to you. Pray your own prayer in response to the Word of the Spirit to you. Offer the following prayer if it helps you express your thoughts to the Lord.

## Prayer of Response

Lord, help us hear the message for us in this report. The people were awakened from their cultural slumber to hear the fire-breathing sermons of John the Baptist. Prophecy unfolded before their eyes in the visage of a man dressed in skins, living an unorthodox lifestyle, sounding forth with the long-awaited voice of one shouting in the wilderness. The proclamations penetrated the air and startled their sense of norm.

Pharisees, unaccustomed to being the ones under condemnation, received scathing judgment. The common people, accustomed to dismissal as being unworthy in God's sight, were given a way into the Kingdom — by repentance. Repentance from what? From not living by the Pharisees edicts? No. They confessed their personal sins and were baptized into a new way of living as beloved children of God, the joy of Abraham. A pathway had opened that circumvented the bondage of the Pharisees' interpretations of the law. People were ushered into a new freedom and Jesus blessed the new way by being baptized in it as well.

Jesus, unknown to many and long forgotten by others as He grew into God's image over in Nazareth, came into their region and was heralded by John as one far more powerful than any that had come before. From a babe to a preacher, Jesus emerged with John's reminders of prophecy to back him. He who had no sin to confess joined with sinners. A window was opened onto a new hope for the world. God has cared. God has heard. God has come with power to baptize and to save by Spirit and fire. You have come to winnow out the false and unfruitful, and to establish what is true and productive in Your sight.

Thank You, God. We welcome Your Son, whom You love and we love. With Jesus we are well pleased. Help us hear the words of warning, though — to not miss this path by having false faith and wrong priorities. What they missed, we could easily miss. The Kingdom of Heaven is near and we don't want to bypass the entry. Help us clear out all that blocks the way for us and for others. Lord, we come to prepare a straight way for the Lord into our everyday lives. Help us live in keeping with the fruit of righteousness You have given us, and that we have sought in turning back to Your ways.

Come, Lord Jesus, come. Baptize. Welcome us sinners. Lead us in the way everlasting. We rejoice to hear the voice calling in the wilderness, Amen.

# Matthew 4

*Read carefully and prayerfully.* Reflect on the truth that speaks most clearly to you. Pray your own prayer in response to the Word of the Spirit to you. Offer the following prayer if it helps you express your thoughts to the Lord.

## Prayer of Response

Jesus, we celebrate Your humanity. You experienced what we know all too well: doubts that assail us when we are suffering. We want to turn things around in our favor by any means we can. We will sacrifice the wrong things for brief relief. We will twist scripture to make it say what makes us feel better and that promises to satisfy our self-aggrandized existence. We make ourselves the center of what matters. We worship what the world adores. We want what the world offers. We put Your love to the test rather than putting the world's siren claims to the test. We ask the big "IF" questions and set the parameters we expect of You: IF You are God, You would do things the way we expect.

Thank You for setting the example for us in refuting doubt and temptation. Thank You that we have the resource that works. Thank You for scripture as the lamp we need for our path. Thank You for the great light that You have shone into our shadows. Thank You for fulfilling Psalm 23 for us — for giving us a way through the valley of the shadow of death. Thank You for coming to us, as You did to humble fishermen looking to the waters for their living.

What was it that made them ready to leave father and boats to follow You? Had they already heard of You — of the preaching, the healing of debilitating and incurable conditions, of the crowds who were following all around the region? However they knew, they were satisfied that the words they were hearing could only come from the mouth of God, and that the acts they were seeing could only come from the hands of God.

We believe, too. You are the Son of God. You have brought the Kingdom of God near. In You, the reign and authority of God have been fleshed out as compassion, love, and mercy. No wonder they followed. We are drawn, too. Help us make the clear-cut choices in our lives as they did — to leave behind what cannot go with us.

In the name of the One who obeyed and spoke every word from the mouth of God. Amen.

# Matthew 5:1-16

*Read carefully and prayerfully.* Reflect on the truth that speaks most clearly to you. Pray your own prayer in response to the Word of the Spirit to you. Offer the following prayer if it helps you express your thoughts to the Lord.

## Prayer of Response

Just as the people of the times in which You lived crowded near to hear You, we come to hear words that ring truer than all other messages. We come to hear messages that touch us where we live; where the hungry seek sustenance; where the poor in spirit seek hope; where those who mourn long for comfort that enables them to laugh and sing again; and where the meek are often left as prey to those who bully them and claim what is theirs.

We come wondering whether we hunger and thirst for righteousness enough to be filled. We listen shyly to the promises of mercy for the merciful, because we know our hearts. If only the pure in heart will see God, what are we to do? If only the peacemakers will be called children of God, how can we be included? We know what it is like to be mistreated, but it's not always because of righteousness or because of You. The reasons are usually much more mundane, selfish, unethical, or profane than that.

This is cause for heart-searching contemplation. Am I "salty" enough? Does my life bring the seasoning of mercy, righteousness, and peace consistently into any corner of the world? Do my deeds reflect and glorify you? I think I know the answer. What, then? I don't want to be thrown out. Thank You that there is a message for me: "Blessed are the poor in spirit, for theirs is the Kingdom of heaven." What a joyful discovery! There is a place for those who recognize their poverty before You, who call out to be filled with Your righteousness, who mourn over the ways in which they fail to live for Your glory.

Thank You that there is a place in Your Kingdom for those who hunger and thirst to be better, even to the point of incurring the judgment and false accusations of others, willing to live as outcasts while knowing themselves to be the children of God. Thank You for welcoming me into the Kingdom of Heaven. I am humbled and grateful — and amazed. Amazing Grace, how sweet the sound as it reverberates in our souls.

We pray in the name of One who came as light shining in darkness and music ringing in our chambers of despair — and who sends us to do the same. Amen.

# Matthew 5:17-26

*Read carefully and prayerfully.* Reflect on the truth that speaks most clearly to you. Pray your own prayer in response to the Word of the Spirit to you. Offer the following prayer if it helps you express your thoughts to the Lord.

## Prayer of Response

Thank You, Lord, for bringing a different word from what we have heard spoken about God and for God. Thank You that the word which You bring reverberates in our hearts with tones of hope, love, compassion, mercy, grace, and righteousness: blessings which are not based on legalistic judgments. Thank You for fulfilling the Law we could never fully obey. No one could. As Peter would testify later, neither the people of that day nor their forefathers could. If they could not, then surely we cannot expect to do so.

I can imagine the hearts that sank when You said our righteousness had to surpass that of the Pharisees and teachers of the Law. I would have felt "sunk" if I had been there. The words sit heavily even now. They were the ones who supposedly had it all right. What a fresh new gospel — that there is a better righteousness within reach of any of us. But we realize that it is not for the faint of heart, either.

While I am happy to obey the commands not to murder, I have been angry with a brother or a sister — or a friend. I may not have called either a "fool," but I have treated them in ways that conveyed that message. The righteousness of reconciliation is within my reach, yet I have a hard time attaining it. It requires eating humble pie. Thank You for raising my awareness that I am out of step with You until I do and that the best time for reconciliation is when I am still in some measure of relationship with the one from whom I am alienated. Thank You for the reminder that alienation grows with each day of delay and needs to be nipped in the bud speedily.

Nudge me forward, Lord. Place Your hands on my shoulders and whisper to me, "I am with You. You can do this. I have paved the way." Help me trust Your Spirit. We pray in the name of the One who reconciles us to God and sends us to do the same. Amen.

# Matthew 5:27-48

*Read carefully and prayerfully.* Reflect on the truth that speaks most clearly to you. Pray your own prayer in response to the Word of the Spirit to you. Offer the following prayer if it helps you express your thoughts to the Lord.

## Prayer of Response

Lord, taken literally, this means that there should be a lot of blind men walking around. And, truth be known, a lot of blind women. In today's world, adultery is almost the status quo and lust is what the world feeds on. It's not just one eye that has sinned but both eyes — perhaps most eyes. It's not just right hands but both hands that need to be sacrificed. Sexual immorality and self-serving divorce are rampant. This is disheartening. No wonder You said that the way into the Kingdom of Heaven is narrow and few will find it.

This way that we walk with You is not as restricting as the Pharisaical Law, but it is not an easy way. We are relieved to give up the ancient "eye for eye" judgment, but we are taken aback by the instructions to give those who slap us another chance, or someone who steals from us another piece of property to go with what has been stolen. Even our choice of words has to change when we walk with You. That, I may be able to manage; but it really takes my breath away to hear that I must not only love my good neighbor but also my enemy. I get it, though. God has done that for me.

When I live like His enemy, He still provides His grace and mercy on me, like rain that showers or sun that warms rocky wastelands as well as fertile fields. When I do not live like a child of God, His perfect love still claims me as His own, still reaches out to reclaim me; He simply wants me to be inclusive in the same way. From that perspective, none of this is too much to ask. Being in Your family, one of Your children, is incentive enough. Perfect Heavenly Father, help me be wholly and completely an ambassador of Your love.

We pray in the name of the One who loves those who don't know they are loved. Amen.

# Matthew 6:1-13

*Read carefully and prayerfully.* Reflect on the truth that speaks most clearly to you. Pray your own prayer in response to the Word of the Spirit to you. Offer the following prayer if it helps you express your thoughts to the Lord.

## Prayer of Response

We need this reminder, Lord. We are in the spotlight all the time. We are seen by You, heard by You, known by You in every move that we make, every thought that we think, and every word that we speak. We may be able to fool some people some of the time, maybe all of the time, but we never fool You. We hear and ponder the message that we never receive Your reward by seeking it publicly. If we want fame or commendation as a reward, we may be able to get it from the world, but it doesn't come from You when we seek it out of selfish motives. Our giving must be like our praying — in secret, where You know us intimately. Where You know our true motives.

So, we come like the disciples, needing to learn how to pray as well as how to live. Even in our praying we can be motivated by self-serving intentions. Help us learn the secret of the inner room — the interior of our lives, where You abide with us and know all of our needs before we ask. There, the Kingdom of Heaven is approached. There, the Unseen meets with us, unseen by the world. There, we know You as Father, *our* Father in Heaven, not just mine but the Father of all.

So, Lord, we pray as You have taught:

Our Father, may Your name be held holy in my life — my thoughts, words, and actions. May Your reign be fully realized in my inner being, and Your yearning love be truly expressed in my life and that of all Your people throughout the created universe and heaven. We look to You for our daily sustenance, aware that everything originates with You. We recognize our failure to fulfill Your righteous purpose in our lives, and our need to forgive and be forgiven. Indeed, we are growing to understand that forgiveness is the central axis for a life lived faithfully to Your glory. Lead us so that we will not fall into temptation, and deliver us from the deadly grasp of evil influence and purpose.

In the name of the One who taught us to pray humbly and honestly, Amen.

# Matthew 6: 9-13

*Read carefully and prayerfully.* Reflect on the truth that speaks most clearly to you. Pray your own prayer in response to the Word of the Spirit to you. Offer the following prayer if it helps you express your thoughts to the Lord.

## Prayer of Response

Our Father who art in heaven, in the secret unseen place, shining in Glorious Light, hidden from our eyes yet revealed in our hearts, Your name is Wonderful. You are God — Creator, Sustainer, Redeemer, Healer, Helper, Defender, Guide, and Friend. You are the Light of the World, revealed through Jesus the Christ, perfect in pure holiness and righteous love.

O Holy One, Mighty God, reign in my life. May Your full sovereign authority be known and obeyed in my thoughts, words, choices, and deeds. Thy will be done in my daily life as in the glorious realm of Your supreme presence, where angels obey You and saints adore You. May this day be my focus, seeking only enough to sustain my life in Your will, ceasing to clamber for more than I need. As You have promised to remember my sin no more, teach me, train me, discipline me to focus on the good in others, and to forgive the bad. As You have always sent Your sunshine and rain upon the good and the bad, I want to bestow kindness on all.

Help me extend the grace and mercy You've shown me, to them — to those who accuse, pressure, misuse, malign, and abuse me. Lead me to live as Christ, through the power of His love, showing "humility in conduct, stability in faith, modesty in words, justice in deeds, mercy in works, strictness in morals, unwillingness to do wrong and willingness to endure wrong. . ."[1] Free me from all that could separate me from You. Deliver me from aligning with evil in the world, from condoning it, or giving it opportunity for expression in my attitudes or behavior. Cover me in Thy atoning grace. Refresh me in Thy unquenchable love. Renew me in Thy resurrection power through the presence of Thy Spirit, even Jesus the Christ.

Hallowed be Your name, O Lord. Amen.

# Matthew 6: 14-26

*Read carefully and prayerfully.* Reflect on the truth that speaks most clearly to you. Pray your own prayer in response to the Word of the Spirit to you. Offer the following prayer if it helps you express your thoughts to the Lord.

## Prayer of Response

Lord, there may be nothing more troublesome for us in life than the need for, and the requirement for, forgiveness. We want to be forgiven, but not if it means repentance. We want to be forgiven, but not if it means passing the blessing on to those who have wronged us. We want peace from regret and guilt, but are reluctant to grant that blessing to others or to make the necessary changes in our lives. We especially do not want to admit any guilt on our part. So, this is a startling declaration and one that we must take to heart: that our eligibility for forgiveness is tied to our compassionate ability to forgive others and to our humility in seeking reconciliation.

Oh, we'll do it when others are watching — if pressed into proving our "Christian love." Like Your admonition about fasting, we forget that the only one who really knows and sees our inner being is also the only one who matters. You know when we forgive from the heart or when we just act nice in person while adding grievances to our tally sheet and barriers to relationship and community. Help us choose to store up the greatest treasure of heaven — forgiveness. There is nothing more valuable and nothing so indestructible. It is the light that chases away all darkness from our hearts and from our view of the world around us.

And forgiveness gives us a whole lot less to worry about! Lord, a lot of our clamoring in life is related to our need to keep up appearances, especially to look good in front of our enemies — as a taunt. Help us learn the lessons of the natural creatures of the world. Like birds, help us greet each day with a song in our hearts, to enjoy the food that is given, to dress for protection more than reputation, and to trust our lives to the upward wind currents of God's spirit.

Glory be to God, Treasure of our Heart. Amen.

# Matthew 6: 25-34

*Read carefully and prayerfully.* Reflect on the truth that speaks most clearly to you. Pray your own prayer in response to the Word of the Spirit to you. Offer the following prayer if it helps you express your thoughts to the Lord.

## Prayer of Response

Lord, I can still see the pillow in my mind's eye. Mother gave it to me when I was a teenager. It was bright red and in bold letters fairly screamed out the admonition: "Don't just sit there! Worry!" In spite of that daily reminder, I worried. It is still my modus operandi, though I know Your words are absolutely true.

Worry has never put more food on the table, poured more water in a glass, put more clothes in the closet, cleaned the house, cultivated the garden, secured a job, passed an exam, restored health, increased life span; and it certainly never added an inch to anyone's stature. Although, it can add inches to our girth, because we tend to eat less nutritional foods and get less exercise when we are depressed. Worrying over anything is a waste of time and a detriment to life. Yet we do it — perhaps as a way to exert at least emotional control over situations. There really is not much in life that we have control over, though we worry as if we do.

Help us learn the lesson of the birds and the flowers, and of each tiny blade of grass brimming with powerhouses of cellular life. Thank You for this reminder that You see value in what we view as small and insignificant, and that no one is of more value than another. You help each one in the same way. Help us understand that life is more than food, clothes, and possessions. It is about fulfilling the purpose of Your will for us — Your yearning love for us. Solomon was able to acquire all he wanted in life, but even Solomon missed his highest purpose by focusing on acquisition, power, and influence. It is easy to get caught up in the pagan pursuits of the world and so miss the higher calling to God's Kingdom and Righteousness.

Help me remember that tomorrow will come even if I don't fret, plan, and worry. Let trouble worry. Let me trust my Maker. Let pagans scramble. Let me seek God's loving purpose. Let temptations lose their influence over me. Let the beauty of simplicity entice me and satisfy me.

Lord, thank You for hearing our prayers — so that we may worry less. Amen.

# Matthew 7:1-12

*Read carefully and prayerfully.* Reflect on the truth that speaks most clearly to you. Pray your own prayer in response to the Word of the Spirit to you. Offer the following prayer if it helps you express your thoughts to the Lord.

## Prayer of Response

Lord, it's interesting that judgment works like forgiveness: what we give is what we get — in equal measure. Sobering. Disconcerting. Disturbing. Thank You for the warning. As uncomfortable as it is, we need to see the logs in our own eyes. While we nitpick at the faults of others, we are blind to our own. When we are finally given a glimpse of ourselves as others know us, it's frightening, so we quickly divert our attention back to their faults. We hide our true identities, even from our own conscious awareness. It's amazing that we can do that, and it's dangerous.

Open our eyes, Lord, to our false selves. Open mine. That is what I ask, what I seek, what I knock on the door of heaven for: to truly know myself and my need for change. I ask for the bread of life, the living Word of God, to nurture me and to grow me into loving interactions with others. I ask for that which will satisfy my soul's hunger according to God's knowledge of me. And I ask for the grace to give to others the good gifts that I seek from them: gifts of compassion, kindness, forgiveness, peace, and mercy.

We pray — asking, seeking, and knocking for Your will and Your way. Amen.

# Matthew 7:13-29

*Read carefully and prayerfully.* Reflect on the truth that speaks most clearly to you. Pray your own prayer in response to the Word of the Spirit to you. Offer the following prayer if it helps you express your thoughts to the Lord.

## Prayer of Response

Lord, the contrast between true and false is sometimes blurred. Clarify our vision of what is true and right, and what is in opposition to Your Kingdom. The false prophets claim to know You or to know one better than You. Help us look carefully to see the wolf fur peeking out from the attractive external coverings. Guide us to notice whether or not the fruit matches the tree. Thank You for the reminder to go to good sources to find the good things You provide. Help us pay attention to what is promised and what is harvested. Strengthen us to resist the urgency to get on board before we know the real inner attributes of those who would entice us into worldly pursuits.

Let me not call Your name in emptiness and futility. Help me remember that we must not take Your name in vain by seeking for anything other than Your will to be done. Help me remember that all the wonders of success that I can put in motion are without substance if I am out of step with You. Help me pay attention to the underlying theology and philosophy of my life and in the lives of others. I don't want to waste my life building that which will not hold up when the storms of life come.

I want to build on the rock of Your Word. I want to hear and put into practice what You outline as essential, for Your words are the only words with real authority. Lord, Lord, may we not call Your name in vain. Amen.

# Matthew 8:1-4, 17; 7:6

*Read carefully and prayerfully.* Reflect on the truth that speaks most clearly to you. Pray your own prayer in response to the Word of the Spirit to you. Offer the following prayer if it helps you express your thoughts to the Lord.

## Prayer of Response

Lord, I come to You as the leper did, saying "if You will, You can make me clean." Forgive my "ifs and what ifs." I come seeking a faith sense to believe, even in this moment, that You are stretching toward me, reaching out to touch my pain, my fear and disappointment, my disease and sin. Speak to my heart those life-giving words: "I will; be clean."

Cleanse my soul and renew my mind. Heal my body and restore a right spirit in me. Help me live with this healing in quiet humility, sharing it with those who ask and seek as well. Help me that I might heed Your warning and not cast my pearls before those You called swine, people who would turn to trample and attack rather than turn to be healed. I do not want to bury this priceless pearl but to share its rare beauty and incomparable value with those who are seeking and needing to know the treasures to be discovered, and cherished, in You, the One who has taken our infirmities and borne our diseases.

In the name of the One who reached out, touched, healed. Amen.

# Matthew 8:1-20

*Read carefully and prayerfully.* Reflect on the truth that speaks most clearly to you. Pray your own prayer in response to the Word of the Spirit to you. Offer the following prayer if it helps you express your thoughts to the Lord.

## Prayer of Response

Lord, faith is the key, isn't it? Why is it so hard to hold? It's the key to the city of God — the key to the inner chamber of prayer where we may commune with You. It's the key to opening the bank of truth in the scriptures and the key to our own healing of mind, heart, soul, and body. Faith is the key that unlocks our fetters that chain us to this world's charms and that enables us to delight first and foremost in You. It is the key to loving You with all my mind, heart, soul, and body.

Over and over You instructed folks, "Go; be it done for You as You have believed." Lord, help me to go forth in faith, confident that all You have revealed and accomplished is fully operational. Help me to believe and to not waver when I see the expanding ocean of unbelief and waves of "intellectual doubt" around me. Help me believe what others may dismiss as scientifically implausible. Heal my paralysis of fear, which prevents me from accomplishing Your purpose in the face of cross-purposes among people with whom I have relationships. Heal me of the fever of discontent that keeps me clambering for satisfaction in things or experiences that will never satiate me. Deliver me from attention to the demonic voices that defy and deny Your goodness and that delight in sensation, seductiveness, and destruction of faith, hope, and love.

Do I dare pray, "May it be done for me as I have believed"? Lord, help Thou my unbelief. Amen.

# Matthew 8:21-34

*Read carefully and prayerfully.* Reflect on the truth that speaks most clearly to you. Pray your own prayer in response to the Word of the Spirit to you. Offer the following prayer if it helps you express your thoughts to the Lord.

## Prayer of Response

Lord, help me overcome fear with faith. Like the early disciples, I have heard Your teachings and have enjoyed close communion with You in prayer — and yet I fall into fear at the sound of danger around me, not unlike Peter trying to walk on water until he saw the threatening waves. Like the disciples in the boat on the storm-tossed sea, I fear You aren't really with me, that You are asleep in the stern and unaware of my calamity. I know that is dishonoring You, yet I am guilty of not fully trusting.

I fear because of deeply embedded distrust. Like the city dwellers who feared the economic impact of following You after demons drove a herd of swine down a cliff, I distrust my life under Your will and ways. I fear loss of control, even though my control has not taken me where I want or need to be. Like the one who wanted to follow You only after getting his life organized, I fear to lay down everything to follow You.

You ask, "Why are You afraid, O child of little faith?" I have no idea, no answer. But my fear is real and remains. It is always under the surface and therefore my #1 enemy. Arise, O Lord, again and command the waves and winds of my fear to subside and cease. Help me remember who You are, believe Your love and power — and trust — really trust. Even the winds and waves obey Your voice. Help the winds and waves of my soul to obey Your voice and thereby find true strength.

We pray in the name of the One who commands our fears to cease. Amen.

# Matthew 9

*Read carefully and prayerfully.* Reflect on the truth that speaks most clearly to you. Pray your own prayer in response to the Word of the Spirit to you. Offer the following prayer if it helps you express your thoughts to the Lord.

## Prayer of Response

Lord, thank You for the gospel that declares that You have compassion for those who are harassed and helpless, those who need guidance and mercy. I find comfort and hope there. You taught Your disciples to care for people who need a kind and wise shepherd, and to pray for workers to go out among them to teach, preach, and heal. So, Lord, I pray for people in churches to be revived in faith and in action that reaches out to care, not to condemn; to teach, not to judge; to heal, not to harm.

Help me understand how I can be a wise shepherd to someone who may benefit from the knowledge of You that I am blessed to have. Help me to believe in and accept Your healing of mind, soul, and body; to exercise faith in order to be able to guide others to trust in Your gracious love. Thank You that it all begins and ends with forgiveness. We all need grace and mercy for our manifold transgressions of thought and tongue, as well as of time and action. I need it and seek it in this moment. Make of my heart a fresh wineskin to be filled with the new wine of Your unconditional love, so that I may readily pour forth forgiveness and mercy to all.

Lord, You asked a good question of the Pharisees, "Why do you think evil in your hearts?" Why do I? Forgive me, for time after time I have entered into the prevailing cultural concepts rather than the truth of Your power and will to forgive, heal, and deliver. I have heard Your call but feared public opinion. I have questioned and criticized when I should have affirmed, encouraged, celebrated, proclaimed, and declared.

I have preferred to socialize with the attractive and affluent, when You would draw aside to dine with the unattractive, unclean, and even despised. You desire to give mercy and You desire for Your people to give mercy, freely and fully, heaped up and running over, not gingerly or guardedly dispensed.

Thanks be to God that You came to call the sick and sinful, because the truth is that I am among them. We all are. So, of course, I should serve You among them. Cleanse me of the misdirected thoughts that obscure and distort reality and muffle Your call. We pray to take heart and spread the good news — because our sins are forgiven. Amen.

# Matthew 10

*Read carefully and prayerfully.* Reflect on the truth that speaks most clearly to you. Pray your own prayer in response to the Word of the Spirit to you. Offer the following prayer if it helps you express your thoughts to the Lord.

## Prayer of Response

Dear Lord, we live in a wide, wild, and wonderful world — of wolves, serpents, and doves; of danger, disease, and delight. Though distorted by the sin and sins of mankind, there is glorious beauty to be seen amidst even the most appalling conditions and calamities. The world is full of magnificent color and design, along with infirmity, death, and demonic forces. There is prejudice and conflict at every hand; help and hope are often in short supply.

You call us to remind everyone wherever we go that there is a life that is different, a higher life we can enter — even the very Kingdom of God. You encourage us to live in conscious awareness of our life in Your Kingdom, paying attention to Kingdom attributes, such as peace, generosity, hospitality, kindness, and health-giving service. And You tell us not to fear in the face of all that the world says and does in confrontation or rejection of Your true way of love. But, we are slow learners.

You assure us that we are of great value to You, yet we fail to fully comprehend this wonderful news. Just as You take note of each sparrow that falls, Your eye is upon us in our calamities and victories. You know every hurt, pain, need, and fear. You tell us to keep our eyes on You and Your higher purpose, and not to be dismayed by all the ranting of those who turn away, or who press us to turn away. Help us loosen our grip on all the earthly, worldly pleasures that we grasp so tightly that we cannot take hold of all the good in store for us in Your Kingdom. Help us find Your eternal life by losing our self-focused life, for the sake of Your truth, righteousness, and glory. Help us live truly as Your disciples in loving care for all.

We pray in the name and power of the One who loved for our sake. Amen.

# Matthew 11

*Read carefully and prayerfully.* Reflect on the truth that speaks most clearly to you. Pray your own prayer in response to the Word of the Spirit to you. Offer the following prayer if it helps you express your thoughts to the Lord.

## Prayer of Response

Lord, Your invitation is exactly what we need and want to hear. We long for someone to take us in, out and away from the elements of life that bind and chafe us, burden and buffet us. We want to lay down our heavy concerns, repeated injustices, failures, fears, and frustrations. We want peace and a reasonable pace in life. We want rest and meaningful productivity. We need truth and wisdom to guide us, and good leaders who build rather than destroy. Help us to learn from You and to accept Your will as our will, and to spread justice and mercy to all.

Help us to be shaped by Your gentle humility. Guide us to take up the responsibilities of Love and Righteousness and to leave behind the burdens of Pride, Covetousness, Prejudice, and Control. Reveal to us Your true nature — Your Love, Wisdom, and Holiness; and mold us into Your image until we do what You would do in care and encouragement for others — the blind, the lame, the sick, the deaf, the dying, and the poor.

Strengthen us to serve You as faithfully as John the Baptist, preparing the way for You in the lives of others by witnessing to our faith in You and Your love for them. May we join those who take no offense in You, who accept You as You are and who repent of personal sins in a sincere quest to live in the will of God by Your teachings. Lord, we come to You, out of our labor and into Your rest, out of our sin and into Your forgiveness, out of our anger and into Your grace, out of our wrangling and into Your peace, out of our fears and into Your strength.

Be Thou our guide while life shall last. Be Thou our eternal home. Amen.

# Matthew 12:1-21

*Read carefully and prayerfully.* Reflect on the truth that speaks most clearly to you. Pray your own prayer in response to the Word of the Spirit to you. Offer the following prayer if it helps you express your thoughts to the Lord.

## Prayer of Response

Lord, thank You for Your tenderness with my brokenness. Thank You that You never shout at me and never bruise me. Thank You that You do not break me, but rather heal me. Lord, my light is smoldering and You tend to it, rather than quenching it. Help me burn brightly for You. Thank You that Your goal is salvation through justice and mercy.

Lift up my eyes to hope in You and to rejoice in Your glory and to live in Your victory. I come to You for healing. I stretch out my arms to You to be strengthened for service. I open my soul to You, for the fullness of Your Spirit to enter. Fill me, and work in and through me to accomplish Your purpose for Your glory.

Help me to discern Your ways of mercy and to follow in the light of Your love, truth, and wisdom. Amen.

# Matthew 12:22-50

*Read carefully and prayerfully.* Reflect on the truth that speaks most clearly to you. Pray your own prayer in response to the Word of the Spirit to you. Offer the following prayer if it helps you express your thoughts to the Lord.

## Prayer of Response

Lord, I have wanted Your will to be done in selected ways, in specific areas for which I have prayed. To live in Your family I see I must seek Your will in all ways. I must be willing to enter into the fullness of Your purpose and close the door behind me, clutching nothing but Your hand. Help me let go of all that will not fit through the door with my hand in Yours. Help me lay it all down at the entrance and never look back.

Help me hear the call of Your family above all other voices. Help me no longer live in separateness and outwardness, apart from You. Draw me into Your inwardness — into the interior life with You that Paul described as "Christ in You" (Colossians 1:27 NIV) and that You described as being "one" (John 17:20-21 NIV) — like that of the Father in You and You in Him. Lead me until I know myself to be *in* You and You *in* me. Keep me *with* You that I may cease to think, do, or say anything that would be against You.

Help me "gather" goodness and love with You, that I may not scatter a trail of discontent behind me. Guard me and teach me so that I will not ever speak against You — Father, Son and Holy Spirit. I want to treasure You, revere You, honor You, and hallow Your name. Show me the good way in all things, that I may store up righteous treasure in my heart and bring forth good fruit for Your glory.

Fill me with Your Spirit until there is no room for lesser influences. Amen.

# Matthew 13:1-23

*Read carefully and prayerfully.* Reflect on the truth that speaks most clearly to you. Pray your own prayer in response to the Word of the Spirit to you. Offer the following prayer if it helps you express your thoughts to the Lord.

## Prayer of Response

Lord, sow the good seed of Your Word in my heart today. Help me be open and responsive to receive the Truth of Your love, and to bear the fruit of love in all my communication and actions. Clear my vision so I may perceive Your presence. Help me hear Your voice and understand Your meaning.

I turn, O Lord, to be healed of my diseases — of mind, soul, and body. Show me the ways I block Your work of Grace in my life. I seek You in faith with the belief that You desire to open the secrets of Your Kingdom to all who turn to You in sincerity. Strengthen my roots in Your Spirit. Rid my soul of the distractions that choke out Your truth and prevent fruitful living.

Shelter and guard me from the scorching, glaring opposition to Your ways that dominates the world around me. Lord, draw me to learn and grow among those whose hearts are not dull, whose ears are not heavy of hearing, whose eyes are not closed; help me perceive, hear, understand, and turn to receive Your blessing.

Make my life a garden that nurtures others in faith, to Your glory. Amen.

# Matthew 13:24-58

*Read carefully and prayerfully.* Reflect on the truth that speaks most clearly to you. Pray your own prayer in response to the Word of the Spirit to you. Offer the following prayer if it helps you express your thoughts to the Lord.

## Prayer of Response

Lord, help me value Your Kingdom of presence enough to sell all that I must in order to claim it. Send forth Your Spirit to help me give up all that hinders me from full entrance. Gather me into Your Kingdom and remove from my heart and mind all that is unrighteous. Help me perceive what is opposed to Your Kingdom and to rid myself of it, to separate the good from the bad in order to fully cherish and treasure my opportunity to live in Your presence now and forever.

Permeate me with Your truth and love, like leaven permeates dough and rises within it, changing it into something of nourishing delight. Forgive me for allowing earthly desires and cultural pressures to choke out Your word of promise. While I was "sleeping," evil was sewn in my heart and mind and is now a part of me. O Lord, please deliver me from my unrighteousness. Gather the weeds out of my life and cleanse me for entrance into Your Kingdom. It is the pearl of great price that I want above all else. It is the treasure I seek.

Please, Lord, do not give up on me and help me to not give up on Thee. Guide me so I will not miss Your gifts, I pray. I am reaching out for Your grace and mercy, indeed for Your redemption, O Christ our Lord. Amen.

# Matthew 14

*Read carefully and prayerfully.* Reflect on the truth that speaks most clearly to you. Pray your own prayer in response to the Word of the Spirit to you. Offer the following prayer if it helps you express your thoughts to the Lord.

## Prayer of Response

Lord, fame is so enticing and debilitating — such a mixed bag. We seek it and envy those who find it — until the haunting paranoia of our departure from God's purpose winds itself around our soul in a relentless death grip. Like Herod, we fear "the people," their opinions and sins, and their judgment of our cultural failings; but we fear Your judgment, too. We recognize that we take joy in the wrong things, only to reap a harvest of regrets. And You wait, until we feel our loneliness enough to call out for You again. You wait, until we will again follow You to find healing and fulfillment.

Break the bread of life to me again and help me follow Your bidding to bless others out of Your supply, multiplied through Your power. Dismiss the crowds and their demands. Restore my soul; refresh, renew, and redirect me on to the next lesson of faith. When I succumb to the apparitions of my fears, remind me that I need have no fear because You are present, all powerful, all wise, and all love. Help me keep my eyes of faith on You, heedless of the pounding of the waves of doubt and the pummeling of the winds of cultural philosophies.

Take my hand when I sink in despair. Lord, save me, for I come to Thee at Thy bidding. Open my eyes that I may truly recognize You and be delivered of the disease and discomfort of my soul and body. O Thou Son of God, Master of the world, Lord of the Ages and Eternal Guide, to Thee be the glory now and always. Amen.

# Matthew 15

*Read carefully and prayerfully.* Reflect on the truth that speaks most clearly to you. Pray your own prayer in response to the Word of the Spirit to you. Offer the following prayer if it helps you express your thoughts to the Lord.

## Prayer of Response

O Compassionate One, who feeds the hungry, heals the sick, and restores sight to the blind, teach us how to differentiate Your Word from the signs of culture. Forgive us when we honor You with our lips but fail to honor You with our lives — and when we pervert the truth to serve our jealousies and covetousness, our traditions and our habits, our selfishness and our self-righteousness.

Deliver us from false worship, blind guides, and petty living. Cleanse us from all impurity that rises within our hearts and finds sinful expression in our lives. Wash us so that we may no longer be defiled. Help us to stand the test of faith and to call upon You as Lord in absolute trust in Your presence, with Your voice to guide us. Help us listen, honor, and obey Your leading.

Strengthen our resolve to reveal Your Word and Your way of love to all. Amen.

# Matthew 16

*Read carefully and prayerfully.* Reflect on the truth that speaks most clearly to you. Pray your own prayer in response to the Word of the Spirit to you. Offer the following prayer if it helps you express your thoughts to the Lord.

## Prayer of Response

Forgive us, O Lord, for we have failed to live in the light of Your power and authority. We have failed to recognize Your divine omnipotence. We have paid more attention to the world around us than to Your world within us. We forget that worry has no place where You reign. We dismiss the critical issues and focus on the trivial.

We look for signs, for clues to guide us, while You *are* the "Sign" for all time. You are the Christ, the Messiah, the One who was and is to come — the Son of the Living God. Yet, we try to lead You to do our will rather than following Your lead. Forgive our shortsightedness — our folly. Help us to forfeit the world's false claims, in order to claim our true life with You. Give us courage to make a clean break with all that hinders us. Help us to bind what needs to be bound, in order to be free to follow You in Your way of grace. Lord, help us recognize the superior efficacy of knowledge in the Spirit above knowledge in the mind.

We pray in the name of the Christ, the Son of the Living God. Amen.

# Matthew 17:1-8

*Read carefully and prayerfully.* Reflect on the truth that speaks most clearly to you. Pray your own prayer in response to the Word of the Spirit to you. Offer the following prayer if it helps you express your thoughts to the Lord.

## Prayer of Response

Lord Jesus, keep me mindful of the brightness of Your glory. I repent, confess, and apologize for looking away and not gazing upon You as the Revelation of God's glory. Like Peter at Your transfiguration, I attempt to converse on a human level, when I need to look and listen in awe — and to live in awe of You, the Beloved Son of God with whom He is well pleased. Lord, with You I am well pleased. With myself, I am not. Transfixed before Your transcendent presence, I recognize the foolishness and futility of so much that I think and do.

(Pause and take time to allow the Spirit to reveal all that needs confession in Your life.)

Forgive me, O Lord. Touch me and renew me. Help me rise without fear or shame to focus on You and You alone. Amen.

# Matthew 17:9-27

*Read carefully and prayerfully.* Reflect on the truth that speaks most clearly to you. Pray your own prayer in response to the Word of the Spirit to you. Offer the following prayer if it helps you express your thoughts to the Lord.

## Prayer of Response

Lord, I come to You as My Rock, the Immovable, Immutable center of Life, where all is Peace, all is Truth, all is Grace, all is Love, and all is Power. I come to draw from the streams of mercy flowing to all who seek You. I come to rest in Your love and to find comfort, healing, and hope in Your embrace. I come to bask in the Light of Truth, to have the dark corners of my life illumined and purged of all that is detrimental to me and to others.

I come to resist evil in all its mutant forms. I come to rest, to be nourished and nurtured in Your Spirit. I come to find direction for the next steps of my life — to look out at a world of need that begins at my doorstep and to see where Your footsteps are leading. I come to take Your hand and draw strength, courage, and the determination to deny myself — to take up my cross and follow You. Lead on, O King Eternal.

Lord, help me wait for understanding to become full before lurching ahead on the basis of partial knowledge. You told the disciples not to witness about the transfiguration until after the resurrection — until the fullness of the gospel had been unveiled. There were still too many unanswered questions and gaps in understanding. There were prophecies yet to be revealed and understood. And there was weakness in faith to be addressed.

Lord, so it is with us, with me. We stand helpless before the great needs around us. We live among and participate in a faithless and perverse generation. We do not have faith to move mountains. We are powerless in the face of illness and distressed in the face of persecution and death. We are fearful about much of life in relation to the world's systems, which grow increasingly more anti-human and anti-God.

Plant us firmly on the Mount of Transfiguration and before the Empty Tomb. Help us to take heart, to grow up in our understanding, and to grasp the power of the gospel to meet the needs in and around us. O Blessed Son of God, correct our short-sightedness and our short-comings. Build up our faith to believe, follow, and reveal Your love, and to trust Your power to overcome sin, disease, and death. We pray, O Christ, with faith as tiny as a mustard seed. We pray in hope as dim as a frosted glass, but we pray. Amen.

# Matthew 18:1-20

*Read carefully and prayerfully.* Reflect on the truth that speaks most clearly to you. Pray your own prayer in response to the Word of the Spirit to you. Offer the following prayer if it helps you express your thoughts to the Lord.

## Prayer of Response

O Lord, we are too concerned with greatness and not concerned enough with goodness. We want independence and reject dependence. In fact, our individualistic spirit abhors dependence. Our productivity-based work ethic despises dependence. We forget we are created beings, sheep in Your Pasture, utterly dependent upon You for every breath we take, every thought we can create, every experience of sight, sound, touch, movement, or speech. Yet, we live determined to build our Kingdom more than to enter Yours. We are curious about Your Kingdom, but committed to our own.

Like Alice in Wonderland, we need to become small in order to enter through the narrow door of humility. When we begin to view others and ourselves as children of Our Heavenly Father, we gain a new perspective on life. We see our common frailty, our need, and our susceptibility to temptation and sin. And our compassion is aroused. It is like the magic potion Alice drank to make her the right size to enter the right door. Lord, help us remember that every other person is a wandering child of God, too — lost or found. Each person is in danger of perishing except for Your grace.

Help us to care for one another, no matter how difficult the work of kindness. Help us live for Your Kingdom, no matter how severe the sacrifice of our personal ambitions and desires. Help us let go of anything that hinders our entrance into Your Kingdom of love and righteousness. And help us assist others in their quest to enter. Help us care enough to reach out to those who fail, rather than turn away in disregard of their spiritual plight; for when we come together in humble faith, we find ourselves within the Kingdom. When we build one another up, we cross the threshold and know Your presence among us, and our presence with You.

Come, Lord Jesus. Lead Your children into Your Kingdom. Amen.

# Matthew 18:21-35

*Read carefully and prayerfully.* Reflect on the truth that speaks most clearly to you. Pray your own prayer in response to the Word of the Spirit to you. Offer the following prayer if it helps you express your thoughts to the Lord.

## Prayer of Response

Lord, we slowly come to realize that the key critical issue for our lives, and truly for the entire world, is forgiveness. Forgiveness is a necessary component of my walk with You for sure. I am dismayed when reminded that our forgiveness is blocked when we refuse to forgive. We are created in the image of a Forgiving Father, whose love is like a nurturing, embracing mother. We distort that image when we insist on our "rights" — when we judge and condemn in the name of "holding others accountable."

When I pray "Forgive me, Lord," I know I must at the same time release my right to blame others for their missteps. I must also pray, "I forgive, Lord" — not once, but without end, without fail. And I must forgive from the heart, as an act of will, in the sense of tender yearning for reconciliation. Help Thou my unbelief and my unwillingness.

Help me grow in determination to exercise courageous love in Your forgiving name. Amen.

# Matthew 18:21-35 continued

Read the verses again, carefully and prayerfully. Reflect on the truth that speaks most clearly to you. Pray your own prayer in response to the Word of the Spirit to you. Offer the following prayer if it helps you express your thoughts to the Lord.

## Prayer of Response

Lord, we circle back to this key passage. In hearing Your answer to Peter about forgiveness, we are left speechless, for it is clear that You hold us accountable for the way we treat others in response to their errors. It is clear that You expect — no, require — us to forgive with the same mercy that we experience in Your grace, a bounteous, compassionate, free, selfless, sacrificial grace. But it is hard, especially in the face of abuse, torture, and murder. Show us how to do this. Oh, that's right — You already have — when You prayed, "Father, forgive them for they know not what they do."

Does that mean that we would not do the despicable things that we do if we fully understood our worth in Your sight and Your indestructible love? Then, forgiveness for us is a real change of mind, as much as of heart. We have to think differently than the culture in which we are shaped. Let me begin by remembering that when I have been wronged, I also have been wrong. Yet I am forgiven and given a fresh new start.

Another truth is inherent here as well. When we criticize, judge, condemn — or even gossip — we have left Your forgiving presence only to dish out the same pain that has been inflicted upon us. When we make excuses for not helping someone, we have forgotten how much we have been blessed when someone helped us when we were lacking solutions or resources. It all goes back to loving others as You have loved us.

It is clear that forgiveness is a multi-faceted choice reflected in our repentance, confession, and humility — and also in how well we fulfill the Golden Rule: "Do to others what you would have them do to you" (Matthew 7:12 NIV). Lord, that is the essence of the gospel, isn't it? WE want and seek grace from You and You in turn send us into the world to live as Your reflections, carrying that same grace into every action, every conversation, and every confrontation. Help us see how each situation is an opportunity to celebrate Your mercy by sharing mercy — by living it out moment by moment.

Lord, have patience with us while we grow in this challenge. Help us soak up Your love until we can release others from all their debt and forgive them from our hearts as an act of will — even of yearning love. But, Lord, we would not stop there. Help us so live that we will never need to be forgiven for hurting or hindering others again. Help us live by Christ's name in love to all. Amen.

# Matthew 19:1-12

*Read carefully and prayerfully.* Reflect on the truth that speaks most clearly to you. Pray your own prayer in response to the Word of the Spirit to you. Offer the following prayer if it helps you express your thoughts to the Lord.

## Prayer of Response

Lord, here we encounter one of our most confusing and contentious issues in life today. In this discussion, as usual, we automatically put our emphasis on sexual intimacy in defining adultery or marriage. In Your holy purpose, revealed in the teachings of Jesus, adultery is broader than that, with roots in mind and heart. It is linked to motives, as well as to actions, which put asunder what God has joined together. It is easy to say that it all goes back to what we believe about the authority of scripture and the meaning it has for us in our time, but we are caught between differing views even in that. We need Your light on this path.

It is easy to reach the conclusion that this discourse established male-female union as what God has purposed and joined together, but it is not easy to live with that conclusion. In today's culture, that is fiery rhetoric and causes much conflict for many whom we want to love and support, but who feel unloved and unsupported. Friends and family, believers and non-believers, find themselves at odds with each other. The laws and pending legislation in our country reflect our struggles and conflict, our inner and outer turmoil over sexual orientation, as well as marriage and divorce.

Then we come to Your discussion about eunuchs. In this, do we find some light that can illuminate a pathway through this morass of indecision and aggressive activism? Is this applicable to our dilemma today? Whatever You meant must hang together with Your discourse about marriage and divorce, since it is all part of the same discourse. Perhaps we need to pay closer attention to what You said about eunuchs: some are thrust into their life situation by birth, some by the influence of others, willingly or unwillingly, wittingly or unwittingly; and some may choose their preferred orientation for various biological, emotional, and social reasons. Perhaps we must first be willing to honestly pray for insight into what You were saying, for it may be far different from our assumptions and deep-seated, entrenched concepts. We don't want to find ourselves on the wrong side of such a critical issue.

There are some certainties: to marry or not to marry is our choice in life, with all its consequences; to remain or not to remain married is our choice in life, with all its consequences. To abstain and live celibate is a choice in life, with all *its* consequences — and it is the choice You made in Your human life. You made that choice for the sake of the Kingdom of God.

Your example sets us free to make our choices for the same purpose — for the sake of the Kingdom of God. We know that is our responsibility before You in all the areas of our lives. It is clear overall that whatever our choice, the goal we must set and achieve has more to do with our relationship with You than it does with sexual orientation. We are to be focused primarily on making choices "for the sake of the Kingdom of Heaven." You said, "The one who can accept this should accept it."

So, our focus must be on what You pointed the disciples toward in the initial discussion — what God has joined together. Perhaps the question for each of us to face is, "What has God purposed and joined together for me in my life?" We need to ask, "What will sustain my life and the lives of my loved ones in the most positive ways?" Perhaps we will be surprised that the answer is much more about the Kingdom of God than about our gender or anyone else's. I suspect the answer is related to God's purpose, revealed in Christ, to transform us into loving agents of peace who help shape a more loving world.

Lord, help us take an honest look at You, Your Word in scripture, the potential results of our actions today, as well as the lessons of history; enable us to make the right choices in our own lives. Help us to believe the truth You have revealed, and to grasp the courage to live by that truth in the most loving and peaceful ways possible. Help us to accept Your true purpose and to make choices that enable us to live at peace with You and with one another, for Your glory.

I wonder, Lord, whether our arrival at the truth to which You point is contingent upon first paying attention to where we are in our relationship with You. I suspect we need to make sure we are positioned, ready to receive the truth as it is, for what it is, and to receive it as the Eternal Word of the Creator, given to us for the good of those whom You love. That may make the greatest difference.

Lord, thank You for the insight You give to all who are ready, willing, and able to receive Your truth into their lives. Help me be among them. Amen.

# Matthew 19:13-15

*Read carefully and prayerfully.* Reflect on the truth that speaks most clearly to you. Pray your own prayer in response to the Word of the Spirit to you. Offer the following prayer if it helps you express your thoughts to the Lord.

## Prayer of Response

Lord, You placed significant emphasis on children in Your teaching. Your teaching syllabus seemed to include them whenever possible. I am struck by how You chose to weave instruction about them into various contexts, including questions about greatness and warnings about mistreatment and misguidance. There was welcome and compassion expressed and demonstrated on the heels of observations and questions about marriage and eunuchs. The setting that strikes me most is in the discourse in Chapter 18 about the shepherd focusing on one lost sheep when he had ninety-nine others. It followed Your admonition not to look down on a single child among them. So, that parable was not intended to be primarily about evangelism and missions, was it? I also see that it is about the care, affirmation, and support of each child in our world. Each one is precious in Your sight.

I hear a call for Your people to direct significant resources and attention to the care and well-being of all children. We are all to be concerned about how our decisions and actions impact them. We are reminded that God knows and cares. Lord Jesus, we come as Your trusting children — weak, unwise, and vulnerable. While Your teachings direct us to respect, cherish, and support vulnerable children as You did, I sense that You were also modeling and instructing us for our relationship with God our Father in heaven. We are comforted by the welcome You extended to the children and by Your instructions not to hinder them. In that, we see the welcome of heaven for all of God's children who trust in Him. Thank You that You break down hindrances so that we may come humbly, like children, full of faith and expectation, trusting in Your love and power to save.

Bless the angels who stand near us all our lives, watching, guarding, and guiding us toward heaven's entrance. Thank You that it is not Your will that anyone would miss Your glory in heaven. Instead, it is Your yearning will for us to make it. Lord, where I am off-track, please lead me back to the right path. Lead us all into the faith community where we will be supported in our journey to heaven. Be in our midst. Shape us into those who belong in heaven, and as those to whom heaven belongs by birthright from our Creator who made us for heaven.

Help us be ambassadors for heaven as we go — especially for the good of the little children, whose souls are still tender toward You. May the example of our lives lead little ones to seek heaven and to discover the welcome there that transcends all other joys. Help us break down hindrances.

In the name of the One who loves the little children, Amen.

# Matthew 19:16-30

*Read carefully and prayerfully.* Reflect on the truth that speaks most clearly to you. Pray your own prayer in response to the Word of the Spirit to you. Offer the following prayer if it helps you express your thoughts to the Lord.

## Prayer of Response

Dear Lord, thank You for the assurance that You make all things, the possible and the impossible, matters of hope for us. Help us set our vision on the right goals. We hear our own prayers in the voice of the rich young man who came to You asking, "What good deed must I do to inherit eternal life?" We also want life at its best as we have envisioned it, and would hope that with just one spectacularly good deed or life practice we could balance the scales to favor our entrance into heaven. We want our cake and to eat it, too.

We gasp at Your answer and are ill-prepared to live totally unselfishly. We can do it in increments or piecemeal: Refuse to kill? — check! . . . Be faithful? — check! . . . Be honest? — check! . . . Be truthful? — check! . . . Be respectful and grateful to parents? — check! . . . Treat others kindly and fairly? — check! . . . But the first four commandments that You did not name — those are the ones that trip us up. Oh, we may be careful not to make or worship handmade idols, and we may be careful not to use Your name flippantly as a curse word or without regard for Your omnipotence and holiness. But we have a deep, underlying awareness that our hearts are not fully, without reservation, focused toward You, O God.

We have areas of holdout. Before we finally forge our commitment, we slink away to think about it more. An all-out commitment is scary. What does it mean, other than what You said? Is it any different in our culture today — in my life — than in that young man's culture? Is there a loophole? O Lord, help me to not be among those who turn aside sorrowfully to ponder, never to act. Help me to truly follow You and to divest myself of all the personal hindrances to life in the Kingdom of Heaven.

Forgive our and my procrastination and presumption of Grace, our excuses for inaction. Help me leave behind, get rid of, repudiate, or sell whatever takes my focus away from the goal of following You in absolute surrender. Help me "love the Lord my God" supremely, and help me see all of my life for what it really is: a part of His Creation. Help me turn a deaf ear and a blind eye to the wanton call of current culture. Help me see beneath the veneer to what really matters.

Make the impossible possible — help me follow You fully, O Christ our Good Shepherd. Amen.

# Matthew 20:1-16

*Read carefully and prayerfully.* Reflect on the truth that speaks most clearly to you. Pray your own prayer in response to the Word of the Spirit to you. Offer the following prayer if it helps you express your thoughts to the Lord.

## Prayer of Response

O Lord, our God who does whatever is right, help us adjust to Kingdom living. Help us to understand where we are in the context of this parable: paupers without meaningful engagement or basic life resources. You have said, "Apart from me you can do nothing." For a self-sufficient people, that is a difficult truth to grasp. We are capable of so much, and accomplish so much, that we scarcely comprehend what You meant. It takes us aback to think that it is possible that all we do, in the long run, could be meaningless. Lord, save us from such an awful peril, for we work hard to be successful in life.

We are not unlike day laborers waiting for an opportunity to do something meaningful, sometimes indiscriminately filling our hours and days with less than fulfilling work, in order to feel productive, or to increase our income. Thank You for taking the initiative, for seeking us out, and providing us with opportunities to be vitally involved in Your purpose. We praise Your deliverance from futile, useless living. We rejoice in Your relentless pursuit of us in Your desire to engage us in a dynamic, fulfilling, fruitful life.

Forgive us when we fail to show up for duty, and especially when we compare our selves and our results to those of others. Keep us focused on our own personal walk with You, gratefully and humbly receiving Your promises to us with selfless indifference to the issues of prosperity. Help us understand that it is easier to live simply than to be always clamoring for more. Adjust our vision to see clearly that no one being is worth any more than another, that all are equal in Your realm. Help us welcome others as having equal value, and help us trust Your grace to be sufficient to meet our shared challenges.

To God be the glory. Amen.

# Matthew 20:17-34

*Read carefully and prayerfully.* Reflect on the truth that speaks most clearly to you. Pray your own prayer in response to the Word of the Spirit to you. Offer the following prayer if it helps you express your thoughts to the Lord.

## Prayer of Response

Lord, it is interesting that when You heard the requests of two different groups, You responded with two different questions. To those seeking power, prestige, and authority, You asked, "What do You want?" But You denied their request. To those seeking to see clearly in order to be productive, You responded with a similar but different question, "What do You want me to do for You?" And You answered their request. Those humbly seeking mercy received the gift of sight. Lord, I choose to be in that group.

I have no desire for power, prestige, or authority. Rather, give me clear understanding and the spiritual vision to see You at work and to follow You. Help me see clearly how to extend grace, mercy, and freedom to all. Release me from the bondage of self-focused religious authoritarianism. Draw me into the marvelous freedom and liberty of selfless indifference to anything but Your will, Your yearning love for our highest good.

Help me serve, whether as a leader or a supporter, with a servant's heart. Amen.

# Matthew 21:1-13

*Read carefully and prayerfully.* Reflect on the truth that speaks most clearly to you. Pray your own prayer in response to the Word of the Spirit to you. Offer the following prayer if it helps you express your thoughts to the Lord.

## Prayer of Response

Lord Jesus, Son of David, Son of God, we are surprised and confused by Your sovereignty. We are dismayed by our helplessness, error, and ignorance before You. Your wisdom and omniscient knowledge astound us. We are intrigued by Your entrance into humanity's experience and history, with the infinite preparation and attention to minute detail in prophecies, people, and places. Your authority catches us in our discrepancies, challenges our principles, and convicts us.

Lord, come to us as You did to Jerusalem. Come in peace and come in power — power to overcome our selfish pride and power to overturn our unrighteous pursuits. Help us surrender our plans and possessions to what You have need of for Your purposes.

Hosanna! King of Kings! Lord of Lords! Jesus of Nazareth! Christ of God! Hosanna in the highest! I open my life to You. I spread my garments of praise and obedience before You. I line the roadway of my heart with them and ask You to come in, cleanse me of all that offends, and renew me as a person of authentic prayer and worship, living and praying in righteousness. Amen.

# Matthew 21:14-27

*Read carefully and prayerfully.* Reflect on the truth that speaks most clearly to you. Pray your own prayer in response to the Word of the Spirit to you. Offer the following prayer if it helps you express your thoughts to the Lord.

## Prayer of Response

Lord Jesus, surely You are God — for Your authority and wisdom astound us. Your power and judgment disturb us. The story of the fig tree rattles us. The Divine perspective perplexes us and unnerves us. Like the fig tree, we fail to produce right fruit at the right time. We, too, are out of sync with the rhythm of Your will. We confess that we care more about keeping our lives on our chosen paths than on Yours.

Like the religious leaders of Your day, we react with questions, doubts, and skepticism. We dismiss the obvious in order to protect our interests. Ultimately, we don't want to miss the truth; yet that is the danger when we focus only on the signs of Your omnipotence that confound our rational minds. Clear our vision, O Lord. Help us to understand Your lessons in faith and to comprehend Your living example of faith.

Keep us mindful that faith is our birthright. You created the world by Divine Faith. You sustain the world by Omnipotent Faith. You judge sin and redeem us by Pure Faith. That is the basis of our faith and the nature of divine authority and of our salvation, sanctification, and glorification with You. Lord, I believe. But — help Thou my unbelief.

I pray for faith to receive whatever I ask in prayer, as outlandish as that sounds to say, even in a whisper; but I pray because You have taught us to pray in that dimension — even for faith to remove mountains. I don't have a literal mountain that I want to move, but there are many situations in my life that I would like to shift. Help me pray by faith with an unselfish desire to produce righteous fruit, and to know assuredly that You hear and answer according to Your will. Amen.

# Matthew 21:28-46

*Read carefully and prayerfully.* Reflect on the truth that speaks most clearly to you. Pray your own prayer in response to the Word of the Spirit to you. Offer the following prayer if it helps you express your thoughts to the Lord.

## Prayer of Response

Lord, I fall on the stone rejected by other builders and I am broken on it. Forgive my duplicity in thought and action. Forgive my sham, my pretense. I need to take my place among the tax collectors and harlots — in repentance, at the waters of baptismal cleansing again — for purification of heart and soul — for restoration of life.

I repent, Lord, and seek Your forgiveness for not believing enough to go and do what You want me to do — for reflecting, even committing, but not acting. Lord, forgive me for fearing opinions and stepping back rather than stepping up to honor Jesus in all situations. Cleanse me of petty pride and fears. Break me open until I see my deeply imbedded unbelief and disobedience. Remold me in Thy image. Fill me with Thy Spirit; teach me and help me to rebuild a life of obedience and true worship. Help me recognize You and never reject You or those You send.

We pray, longing to be people who produce the fruit You desire. Amen.

# Matthew 22:1-14

*Read carefully and prayerfully.* Reflect on the truth that speaks most clearly to you. Pray your own prayer in response to the Word of the Spirit to you. Offer the following prayer if it helps you express your thoughts to the Lord.

## Prayer of Response

Lord, I fear the outer darkness where You are absent and where evil reigns; where regret consumes the soul and tortures the mind; where anger and evil multiply — creeping, leaping, and consuming all in its path. I fear it and pull back from the edge of it; I ask You to forgive my slights and offenses toward You and Your people. Hear my prayer for deliverance from judgment yet again. I want to be in Your presence, Lord — to find a place set with my name on it at the marriage feast, to be in the glorious union of the Son of God with the redeemed of all the ages.

I want to be among them; but I imagine them to be at a superior level of sanctification, for I am conscious of what I lack. Help me hear the call as they did, above the din of work or play, of friend or foe, of scoffers or zealots, pain or ecstasy, failure or success. Forgive me for making light of Your call in the past or even in this moment — for failing to give that call the highest priority — for deflecting and delaying. Lord, thank You that both the good and the bad may come to Your table. I want to come clothed in the righteousness You require; taking courage in Your grace, I seek the garments of faith and praise. Lord, I raise my hands toward You in worship and in need.

Please call on me and choose me to enter Your Kingdom, not because I am worthy, but because You provide the righteousness I need. Amen.

# Matthew 22:15-46

*Read carefully and prayerfully.* Reflect on the truth that speaks most clearly to you. Pray your own prayer in response to the Word of the Spirit to you. Offer the following prayer if it helps you express your thoughts to the Lord.

## Prayer of Response

Jesus, Son of God, rescue us from our questions — and our answers. Wake us from our sleep of complacent confidence that we already have the answers. Look into our hearts and reveal our error. Show us how we, too, can be wrong because we do not truly know the scriptures or the power of God. We cycle from one round of questions and groups with answers to another, and never fully arrive at all the truth. We are vagabonds, picking up tidbits here and there, never knowing full sustenance.

Even though Peter had a glorious epiphany of insight and declared, "Thou art the Christ, the Son of the Living God," we live as if we had not heard that message. Our ears hear marvelous things that our minds dismiss and our hearts miss — such as: "Behold the Lamb of God that takes away the sin of the world" (John 1:29). It doesn't sink in; so like the Pharisees and Sadducees of old, we search the scriptures only to find questions and conflicts that stump us. We don't want to miss the Son of God and the answers, as well as the peace, though. Teacher, teach us the way of God in all its dimensions. Amen.

# Matthew 23

*Read carefully and prayerfully.* Reflect on the truth that speaks most clearly to you. Pray your own prayer in response to the Word of the Spirit to you. Offer the following prayer if it helps you express your thoughts to the Lord.

## Prayer of Response

Lord, it is sobering to think about — that no one escapes Your judgment. You spoke to the crowds and to the disciples with that message — and outlined a view of God's assessment of each person as well as of the collective world. It takes our breath away. It catches us all red-handed. The most alarming message of all is that the sins of the ages become our sins when we develop similar motives for our actions.

We wince to realize that even some of our church practices fall under the same condemnation as those for which You rebuked the scribes and Pharisees. It is easy to think this only applies to formal religious leaders, or to the people of that day and that ancient religious/political culture. But, when our attitudes are similar, the results of our actions are the same: people are misled, oppressed, dismissed. Lives are diminished when a few are exalted. Lord, help us choose to be servants ourselves, for when we choose otherwise we unwittingly make servants of others. When we exalt ourselves, or accept exaltation of title or status, we demote someone else. This idea is hard, for it cuts across the grain of our most revered and ingrained social and religious customs.

How did we get so far off base? Forgive us for rationalizing and shielding ourselves from the penetrating beam of true righteousness. Forgive us for leading folks astray, for perverting true values, and for missing the true essence of what we are supposed to be about. Cleanse us today. Awaken us and reveal the putrid interior of our polluted minds and hearts. Help us refocus our gaze until all that is impure is burned away. Help us find the courage to turn to You, with the full commitment of our lives and of our very being, to true forms of worship and true actions of justice, mercy, and faith.

Help us escape being sentenced to hell, by admitting — to ourselves, to You, and to one another — our individual and collective guilt. Help us to recognize duplicity in motives, and to be single-minded in our commitment to pure, cleansing righteousness before You.

O Lord, Blessed are You who have come in the name of the Lord to rescue us from our sin. Like people marooned on a raft in a raging sea, we call out to You to take us in Your arms and lift us out of our danger and despair. Cleanse us so that we may be gathered to Your side. Help us to not gloss over a single erroneous thought or deed, but to expose everything to Your purifying gaze until we commit ourselves to full repentance and absolute purity in all we do.

Nothing else matters and nothing else satisfies and nothing else escapes judgment. We are in great need, O Lord, for we are way off base. Help us overcome the strong pull of pride and prejudice, for the world's sake, for our sake, and for Your glory. Amen.

# Matthew 24

*Read carefully and prayerfully.* Reflect on the truth that speaks most clearly to you. Pray your own prayer in response to the Word of the Spirit to you. Offer the following prayer if it helps you express your thoughts to the Lord.

## Prayer of Response

Lord, help us keep in mind the transient nature of all things that we see and value with pride. Help us remember that nothing in this world is permanent. Our mightiest buildings, systems, monuments, bridges, and highways will one day give way to storm, erosion, neglect, or destruction. Help us focus on what matters most. Lift our understanding of our responsibility to live by faith in Your ultimate triumph.

Keep us mindful of our dire need to focus on You and Your Word, remembering that You have already come and are with us in the Spirit, so we have no need to get distracted by news of a messiah or prophet, earthquake or war. Take away our fear and grant us wisdom as we face a world or life spiraling out of control. Help us take courage in Your eternal power and Your promise to deliver the elect from ultimate destruction. Help us choose to answer Your call of election to a place in Your Kingdom.

Raise our awareness and anticipation of Your coming, as we remain faithful to nurture one another in faith, hope, and love. Amen.

# Matthew 25:1-13

*Read carefully and prayerfully.* Reflect on the truth that speaks most clearly to you. Pray your own prayer in response to the Word of the Spirit to you. Offer the following prayer if it helps you express your thoughts to the Lord.

## Prayer of Response

Lord, I come to You with the excitement and reverent anticipation akin to those preparing to attend a great ceremony for a beloved person, like a bridesmaid attending the wedding of her brother. Your parable warns us to come prepared — and to not make assumptions about place or privilege. The odd thing in this parable is that the wise maidens did not share. That rubs against the grain with our inherited view that You would have us share freely. How do we reconcile this?

Help us view life with Your wisdom and know when to let people own their own mistakes and consequences. And help us face our own mistakes and consequences with clear, honest vision and humility.

Lord, Lord, please open the door to us yet again. Forgive our lack of focus and preparation. Guide us by Thy Holy Spirit to recognize the great privilege and potential of communion with You in time to prepare ourselves for Your coming, today and in all eternal days. Amen.

# Matthew 25:14-30

*Read carefully and prayerfully.* Reflect on the truth that speaks most clearly to you. Pray your own prayer in response to the Word of the Spirit to you. Offer the following prayer if it helps you express your thoughts to the Lord.

## Prayer of Response

Our Father who art in heaven, we have such a limited, warped view of who You are and what Your Kingdom requires. We see You through the only lens we have: the ways that the idea of God was presented to us in our faith formation. Unfortunately, we have a cloudy view. Help us see You with fresh vision as we fall prostrate before You in humble admiration and deep, sorrowful contrition for our misplaced fears and lack of devotion.

May Thy name and Thy works be glorified through the thoughts of my mind, the meditations of my soul, the words of my lips, and the works of my hands. Where I have faith, help me share the knowledge of You with others. Where I have received Grace, help me extend mercy to others. Where Your love comforts me, help me affirm and support others. Where Your truth enlightens me, help me spread the Light of Your Word into all the dark corners of ignorance and heresy. Where I have health, abilities, skills, and blessings, help me contribute toward good in the world — for Your glory and Joy in Your Kingdom.

Where I rejoice in hope, help me lift the fallen and fearful on to Your firm, secure foundation. Amen.

# Matthew 25:31-46

*Read carefully and prayerfully.* Reflect on the truth that speaks most clearly to you. Pray your own prayer in response to the Word of the Spirit to you. Offer the following prayer if it helps you express your thoughts to the Lord.

## Prayer of Response

Lord, You have called us to love God supremely and to love others seriously. You even taught us to love others as we each love ourselves. But many of us hang up right there. We don't love ourselves as You do. Many of us feel that we are among the "least" — though we have been created in Your image. WE feel insignificant, unwelcomed, and endangered. We hunger for love and significance in our families and circle of friends. We hunger for Your love. We thirst for the living water of Your Spirit to refresh and renew our hope.

We need to know, with a deeper sense of the reality of it, that You welcome us, forgive us, and ever guide us. We need healing grace, mercy, and compassion to comfort us and to strengthen our confidence. We are sick in sin, imprisoned by the innate sense of failure and the fears that slip in to our lives from our families of origin and from the surrounding culture, and remain coiled in our souls.

Help us to be good to ourselves as You have been — to experience Your cleansing and to be clothed in Your righteousness. We come to Your Word, hungry and thirsty for grace and mercy. We come to drink deeply of Your life-giving truth. We come to know You and to welcome You as Lord. We come to be nurtured in faith, hope, and love. We come to be healed from the damage caused by family, friends, and foes. We come to be freed from the bondage of criticism and excessive expectations.

Lord, please do not separate us from Your presence, for we are here and we want to fulfill Your will. We do not intend to join those who fail to answer Your call, so please open Your arms to us and prepare us to share Your welcome with others. Show us how to love each person, one person at a time, giving of our resources and ourselves — giving the marvelous gift of time.

Lord, lead us in ways that engrave Your image on us until we are able to reflect Your love to others. Amen.

# Matthew 26

*Read carefully and prayerfully.* Reflect on the truth that speaks most clearly to you. Pray your own prayer in response to the Word of the Spirit to you. Offer the following prayer if it helps you express your thoughts to the Lord.

## Prayer of Response

Lord, how little we know ourselves and how little we know You. After hearing this passage many times over the years, the truth remains shrouded in mystery. This story that shapes us also mystifies us. It terrifies us as it convicts us and draws us into it. We recognize the cunning and deceit, and we know that we, and those around us, share in that guilty behavior.

We recognize the merciless, hard-hearted criticism. We have experienced its hurtful sting and caused its hurtful sting. We get our values topsy-turvy, too. We betray You by our words and actions whenever we claim to be Christian and yet live outside the truth You revealed. We deceive ourselves with our own cleverness in an attempt to follow, while eluding the consequences of full-scale discipleship.

While You and others suffer for righteousness, we keep our distance, protected from real identification and participation. We are drawn to You, in awe of You, but afraid of the consequences if we give full-scale devotion to You. We sleep and take our rest while evil, cloaked in the guise of a friend, gets the upper hand. We wear that guise as well. Forgive us, Lord. Help us live honestly and wholeheartedly for You.

May the bread of the new covenant feed us with true righteousness. May Your blood of the new covenant fulfill the purpose of its outpouring: to save us from our sins. May our lives become as precious ointment poured out in sacrificial love for You and for all whom You love. May our prayers be attentive to Your Spirit in the will of the Father. Amen.

# Matthew 27

*Read carefully and prayerfully.* Reflect on the truth that speaks most clearly to you. Pray your own prayer in response to the Word of the Spirit to you. Offer the following prayer if it helps you express your thoughts to the Lord.

## Prayer of Response

Lord, I sense a holy aura as I come to this chapter. Here is the critical point for all people. What took place here, when viewed through the lens of all of scripture and of our personal and corporate histories, is of utmost significance to anyone who treads into this majestic account. For the "well" who need no physician, this is a revelation of Your compassion, mercy, and selfless love. For the sin-sick souls, who know all too well a wretched unworthiness before a Holy God, this is their liberation and deliverance, as symbolized in the Old Testament atonement rituals.

Ancient scripture came to mind for the people viewing the scene — they remembered Elijah. The disciples saw prophecies come alive, as in Psalm 22. The words of Jesus fell into place like the pieces of a jigsaw puzzle. The verse that echoes in my mind is Romans 6:23: "The wages of sin is death." Though that is the Divine verdict established in the Old Testament, here the sinless Son of Man and Son of God hangs on a tree, acquitted by Pilate but not released. Here, the unimaginable unfolds and a known criminal is released, while one without sin tastes death, which belongs only to those who sin.

I am amazed that the worst is set free while the best is condemned to death alongside common sinners, even criminals. The light of hope, in the words of Isaiah, slowly dawns: "But he *was* wounded for our transgressions, he *was* bruised for our iniquities: the chastisement of our peace *was* upon him; and with his stripes we are healed. . . and the Lord has laid on Him the iniquity of us all" (Isaiah 53: 4-5 KJV).

Only our sins could claim the life of the sinless One who could call on twelve legions of angels and be triumphant over his enemies. As Paul concluded, our sins were nailed to the cross when Your hands and feet received the spikes (Colossians 2:14). Lord, this is beyond our full comprehension. I can understand that some call it substitutionary and reject it. I wonder if it is because they are well and so can see no need for atonement — and cannot reconcile it with their view of God. I can understand that some are offended by the bloodshed and the idea of atonement from the viewpoint of a satisfying judgment made by a demanding God.

But, I see it from another angle. I fully understand that, for the "sick" who are damaged by a profound sense of unworthiness, it is the only truth that allows us to believe our sins are truly and irrevocably removed — taken away in the Old Testament sense of the scapegoat, driven outside the camp and into the wilderness, never to return. A better sacrifice, one that will never need to be repeated, has been made, not because You are an angry God, but because You love us enough to commit the ultimate sacrifice in order to convince us that our guilt has been completely erased. Our sense of deserved justice and our sense of condemnation is satisfied, not the demands of an angry God.

The Barabbas in each of us is most certainly released. When this sinks in, we can abandon our crutches that we depend on to deal with our anxieties. Thanks be to God through Jesus Christ our Lord, we are truly and eternally set free. Amen.

# Matthew 28

*Read carefully and prayerfully.* Reflect on the truth that speaks most clearly to you. Pray your own prayer in response to the Word of the Spirit to you. Offer the following prayer if it helps you express your thoughts to the Lord.

## Prayer of Response

Lord, I praise You for Your authority, in heaven and on Earth, to dispel doubt, instill truth, and quell fear. I praise You for Your power over nature, sin, and death. I thank You that those who seek You have no reason to fear. Thank You that the Word of heaven is "do not be afraid" for all those who seek Jesus, who was crucified and has risen as He said. Thank You that we can count on all He said and all He did as the core truth and the foundation for our lives.

We turn to join those who worship You, see You, hear You, and know You — and to join those who obey Your call to help others come to believe You and follow Your teachings. O Lord, that is when we come down from the mountaintop. The dazzling light and glistening raiment is gone. People with doubts, fears, and sins abound — people spreading lies, teaching error, hating and hurting one another. Help us keep our eyes on You, to remember who You are and what You have done. Help us go forth in full, joyful confidence that You are always present with us, to help us teach others, and to bring others into full fellowship and faith in the Father, Son and Holy Spirit.

We pray in the name of the Only Resurrected One, Amen.

## Note

[1]T. Herbert Bindley, *St. Cyprian on the Lord's Prayer: an English translation with Introduction* (New York: Edgar S. Gorham, 1914), 43.

# *Praying Through Mark*

## Mark 1

*Read carefully and prayerfully.* Reflect on the truth that speaks most clearly to you. Pray your own prayer in response to the Word of the Spirit to you. Offer the following prayer if it helps you express your thoughts to the Lord.

### Prayer of Response

Lord, Jesus Christ, Son of God, the gospel is still so mysterious to us. We come to this earliest account — the "beginning" of the gospel — and we wonder. We wonder at the marvel of the coming of the Son of God. It is hard to read this from the beginning because we look at it from the end, from the cross and empty tomb and two thousand years of church and world history. But we need a new beginning, and we want what is offered here. We want baptism with the Holy Spirit, prophesied by John the Baptist.

We want to hear God say to us also, "You are my beloved child; with thee I am well pleased." We want to enter the Kingdom of God — to be freed from the hold that worldly evil has on us. We want healing for ourselves, for our loved ones, and for all who seek You for it. Your teaching and healing became a mighty net, drawing multitudes to You. Today we are impotent to heal others or to draw multitudes to You. The healing we seek for others and ourselves eludes us. We confess our need to go back to the beginning and to renew our confession, our repentance, and our faith in You, the Source of all truth and well-being.

Help us understand, believe, and accept the true gospel. Catch us in Your net of love; have compassion and mercy on us. Come to us again,

teaching and healing with authority. We need more than a record of scripture in which to marvel. We need Thy presence and power to wash over us
in forgiveness and healing — to immerse us, flood us in the Holy Spirit.
So, we begin at the only place we can—where the people began in that day
when they first heard of You. We come searching for You. We come praying.
We come to be emptied of all that is offensive to You. We come in faith to
hear, "I will; be clean."

     We come also to be heard. We come to rejoice and go forth with our
own evidence of the gospel at work in our lives. Help us cast the net with
You, not for showy reputation but that others may be caught up in the mystery that welcomes us and assures us, draws us and renews us. We can't go
back. We have seen You, heard You, felt You. We have been caught by Your
love. Here we are. Fulfill Your gospel in us for Your glory. Amen.

# Mark 2

*Read carefully and prayerfully.* Reflect on the truth that speaks most clearly to you. Pray your own prayer in response to the Word of the Spirit to you. Offer the following prayer if it helps you express your thoughts to the Lord.

### Prayer of Response

Lord Jesus Christ, Fisher of Men, all we who believe You gather around You, seeking to be at home with You. We come to hear Your Word, receive Your forgiveness, know Your authority, and be restored, healed of the paralysis in our souls. We come to follow, though we come as sinners in search of Grace. We know ourselves to be unworthy followers, but that is why we follow — to be cleansed from our unworthiness.

O Great Physician, look upon our sin-sick souls and heal us. May Your healing love permeate soul and body, and bring us to rejoice in Your presence and power like those at the wedding party, caught up in the euphoria of fresh love and commitment. Thank You that we have no religious requirement to fast in order to be saved, but only to draw closer to You — to be with You. We rejoice to know that You will not be taken away from us, so our fasting need not be for mourning. All our spiritual practices are undergirded by confidence in Your loving presence.

Pour the new wine of Your Spirit into the freshly prepared wineskins of our souls. Feed us with Your bread of presence — Thou who are King of Kings, God's Anointed, The Great High Priest, Son of the Creator and Agent of Creation.

Let us live in Your rest, to the honor and glory of Your omnipotent name. Amen.

# Mark 3

*Read carefully and prayerfully.* Reflect on the truth that speaks most clearly to you. Pray your own prayer in response to the Word of the Spirit to you. Offer the following prayer if it helps you express your thoughts to the Lord.

## Prayer of Response

Lord Jesus, Son of God, we long for Your family. We want to be among those who do the will of God, the identifying mark of Your "brothers and sisters." But, our lives more often resemble those of the bewildered multitudes who pressed around You. When we look in the mirror of the gospel accounts, we see the dichotomy between who we are and who You call us to be. We stretch out our withered souls and ask to be restored. We turn to You in our dis-ease and with our unclean spirits, unable and unworthy to make You known. Heal us, too.

Whether we are called to preach and cast out demons or to support the work of those who do, we who seek You have much interior and exterior work to do. We have divisions and inconsistencies to be repaired and reconciled. There are pockets of hardness in our hearts sufficient to incur Your anger. Lord, we are arrested in our tracks at Your words, especially at the possibility of committing an eternal, unforgivable sin. Can that happen? We know we are only one step removed from the wandering, fickle multitudes, the judgmental Pharisees, the blaspheming crowds. Have mercy on us, O Lord.

We recognize the precipice and stretch out our hand to grasp Your firm grip of love, love that triumphs over judgment. We want to fulfill the will of God in righteousness. Fill us with Your Spirit; forgive and cleanse us until the words of our mouths, the meditations of our hearts, and the actions of our hearts are pleasing to You, O Lord, our God. Amen.

# Mark 4

*Read carefully and prayerfully.* Reflect on the truth that speaks most clearly to you. Pray your own prayer in response to the Word of the Spirit to you. Offer the following prayer if it helps you express your thoughts to the Lord.

## Prayer of Response

Lord, thank You for ears to hear. Let me hear Your Word to me this day and every day. Sow the good seed of Your Word in my heart. I have chosen to be among those who circle about You seeking the secrets of the Kingdom of God. I come to hear, to accept, and to share the truth, so that others may enter the realm of Your wisdom.

There are many points of connection between my life and the parables. Distractions, like the birds, pick off the seeds quickly so that only a few sprigs take root, and even those become easily scorched in the heat of the day. I have not broken up the soil of my soul enough. I find some protection in the hardness of the hurts that have been packed down until they become a barrier of numbness to more pain. There are imbedded rocks that hinder the deep planting of truth. Grace can't penetrate. Wisdom can't grow. There are too many other desires and intentions crowding out Your Word.

Though I long for Your Word and receive it with joy, I fall away. I stuff it back just as readily and hide it for another day, to contemplate on it, but never to act on it. O Lord, may the seed of Your Kingdom spring forth in the cracks and crevices until it fills my whole heart. Thank You for tending it day and night, from seed to blade to ear to grain to harvest. Thank You that no storm of life can ultimately wipe out Your harvest.

Lord, I fall down before You whom the wind and seas obey and ask that You cultivate a fruitful harvest in me yet. Amen.

# Mark 5:1-20

*Read carefully and prayerfully.* Reflect on the truth that speaks most clearly to you. Pray your own prayer in response to the Word of the Spirit to you. Offer the following prayer if it helps you express your thoughts to the Lord.

## Prayer of Response

Lord, these accounts are so far removed from our comprehension that we wonder what we can glean from them for our lives. In our scientific/ medical context, health issues are explained biologically and treated chemically. Many doubt the reality of demons, but we do know that there are people who get into a state of demonic mind in which their actions and their health seem completely out of control. People can embody evil characteristics today, too. Like this man, to some degree they can know You, worship You, pray and identify their problem. But they can't extricate themselves from their bizarre and destructive behavior alone. In lesser ways, we are all Legion — with many influences that have shaped us and that control our thoughts, words, and actions. Lord, we humbly ask that we, too, may be delivered of our demons.

Drive the ungodliness out of our minds and hearts. Help us find deep compassion for those who are bound in mental and emotional illness. Open our eyes to ways we can support humane care for them and to help them develop a meaningful faith walk with You, until they are able to tell all of their friends how much the Lord has done for them. May we live in gratitude for the blessing of a healthy mind. May we proclaim assuredly how You have had mercy on us and how you have power to save us all from our demons.

When some insist on not hearing the good news, help us to insist on sharing it near and far to those who want to hear. There is good news that needs to be heard — of deliverance from mental and emotional agony through a right relationship with Jesus. Thank You that You still give Peace. Thank You for assurance of forgiveness, love, and salvation. Thank You for guidance, deliverance, and protection. Thank You for Your presence living within and among all who call upon Your name.

May Your love and compassion comfort all who mourn. Depart not from us, O Lord, but stay with us until the ways of God come into glorious focus, and the voices of faithlessness and godlessness depart. Amen and Amen.

# Mark 5:21-43

*Read carefully and prayerfully.* Reflect on the truth that speaks most clearly to you. Pray your own prayer in response to the Word of the Spirit to you. Offer the following prayer if it helps you express your thoughts to the Lord.

## Prayer of Response

Lord, these three stories reveal to us the need for the wisdom to know when to speak and when not to speak. The demoniac was to speak of his deliverance in his home context. The woman healed of the hemorrhage was not allowed to keep it secret, though it was a very personal and embarrassing issue. The family of the child raised from the dead was to keep it secret and just return to normal life, letting the child's health speak volumes. So, how are we to know what to share and when?

Help us be sensitive to the ramifications of speaking the truth in different contexts. Enable us to discern when proclamation will be fruitful and when it will not, and when to let actions speak louder than words. There are people "at home" who could benefit from knowing what the Lord has done for us — and what He can do for them. There are friends who need to know that they can still call on the Lord in faith and find new well being and peace. Help us ignore the forces and voices of unbelief; strengthen us to stifle fear and to believe in Your loving response to our deep and fervent prayers.

At home and away, I want to honor You and to share the joy of walking with You. Fill me with Thy Spirit of love until I overflow in words and actions that encourage others to trust and follow You. Amen.

# Mark 6

*Read carefully and prayerfully.* Reflect on the truth that speaks most clearly to you. Pray your own prayer in response to the Word of the Spirit to you. Offer the following prayer if it helps you express your thoughts to the Lord.

## Prayer of Response

Lord Jesus, Son of God, have compassion on us in our times; we are like sheep without a shepherd, like boats that have lost their moorings. We have forgotten we have a good shepherd who leads us in paths of righteousness, beside still waters of mercy, into green pastures of nurture. We need preachers and teachers to redirect us — apostles sent out by You with the power to cast out demons and to heal the sin-sickness in our minds, souls, and bodies. But first, we need to shed our disbelief and to tear down the barriers of intellectualism and materialism that put science and politics before faith and righteousness.

Lord, come to us. We are making headway, painfully, tossed to and fro among many ideologies. Everyone has an argument that makes enough sense to unsettle us. Atrocities and injustices are being committed in every arena and laws are being made to legalize sin of every imagination. Truth is distorted, turned inside out and upside down, until we don't know what is right. We need prophets. Send them out two by two into all the highways and byways. Astonish us all with the truth in fresh ways. Take our breath away. Break through the defenses of our hardened hearts. We need Your wisdom to guide us. We need Your mighty works to support us. We are no match for the evil of our world.

We confess that we opened the doors to it and are now in bondage to it — misshapen by it. Help us, O Lord. Set us free again. Send Thy Spirit again. Give us authority over the unclean spirits that wreck our lives and relationships. Raise up among us preachers and teachers proclaiming that men and women should turn back to the true and right ways — and make the way clear for others to find and follow. Pass among Your people, healing all who reach out to You in faith and who take no offense at You.

Feed all who hunger and thirst for true knowledge and righteousness. We turn to You, to draw us away from the crowds, and we trust in You. Teach us, Lord. Feed us, Lord. Heal us, Lord. Send us, Lord, two by two, with the good news of Your power to set us on the right course. Amen.

# Mark 7

*Read carefully and prayerfully.* Reflect on the truth that speaks most clearly to you. Pray your own prayer in response to the Word of the Spirit to you. Offer the following prayer if it helps you express your thoughts to the Lord.

## Prayer of Response

Lord, help me not be guilty of false purity, cleaning surface grime while hiding inner filth. I don't want to be defiled on the inside or dishonest on the outside. May my lips and hands be motivated by a heart in love with You and Your righteous ways. Help me discern the difference between Your doctrines and empty human precepts, between Your commandments and human traditions, between Your guidance and human inclinations. Warn me when I tend to put tradition before right and true obligations.

Drive out the "demonic monkeys" that have inhabited our thoughts and expressed themselves in impatience, prejudice, misplaced anger, self-preservation, defensiveness, self-adulation, and jealousy. Yes, Lord, even the dogs under the table eat the children's crumbs. In our times, we need healing, too. Our children need healing. Our ears need to be opened to hear Your voice. Our tongues need to be loosened to speak Your truth. Our eyes need to be opened to see Your path when it differs from our own.

By the Grace of heaven, take me aside and open my eyes, mind, ears, and mouth to see You more clearly, follow You more decisively, hear You more certainly, and to proclaim You more surely. May nothing I do or say make Your Word void to another person.

Astonish us beyond measure, we pray. Reward our faith today, we ask in Jesus' Name. Amen.

# Mark 8

*Read carefully and prayerfully.* Reflect on the truth that speaks most clearly to you. Pray your own prayer in response to the Word of the Spirit to you. Offer the following prayer if it helps you express your thoughts to the Lord.

## Prayer of Response

Lord, we are rendered wordless in the face of Your Word. We are helpless under Your righteous judgment. Indeed, we can do nothing to regain our lives from the world. Only Your Spirit can rescue us away from the side of unbelieving, careless humanity. We live in a world turned upside down, where right is considered wrong and wrong is treated as right. It is hard to keep a true perspective. It is as if we ourselves see a distorted reality and need the rectifying touch of Your power to see all things clearly. Help us gain clarity into the true reality of what matters, and to deny ourselves the pleasure and pride of all that opposes You in both subtle and obvious ways.

As You remained committed to truth and love even when You were beaten and condemned to death, may we take up the commitments we need to keep in the face of enticing allurements and negative, threatening odds. Help us keep the life You have won for us untarnished. Help us face no shame before You, though all humanity may try to break us down with the shame they should own. Help us live on the side of God, acting out of compassion to all, in all situations. Help us deny ourselves pride that puffs up and bars us from simple faith in You.

We commit ourselves afresh to trust Your provision for all our days, and to share as generously when resources are low as when goods are plentiful. Keep us looking intently at You until our view is clear — until we can see that the physical and temporal are secondary, although an important and vital part of our lives. Help us to take heed and to not allow the world to take away what is primary — that You, O Jesus, are the Christ, the Son of God and the Son of Man, raised from the dead and victorious over our death.

You hold the keys of God's Indestructible Life and gladly open the door for us to enter. No other Kingdom is worthy of the full devotion of our lives. May only the glory of God and the holy angels dazzle our eyes and gain the dedication of our souls. Amen.

# Mark 9:1-32

*Read carefully and prayerfully.* Reflect on the truth that speaks most clearly to you. Pray your own prayer in response to the Word of the Spirit to you. Offer the following prayer if it helps you express your thoughts to the Lord.

## Prayer of Response

Lord Jesus, be transfigured before us in Your glory. Help us understand that the Kingdom of God is here with power — and that all who live and die in You are always and eternally with You. Yes, that is our sure hope; but we are like the nine disciples at the bottom of the mountain, dumbfounded and impotent before seeming impossibilities, confused in the midst of clamoring crowds, rattled by arguing scribes who know the words of scripture but miss the True Word.

We all miss the mark until we finally seek no one but Jesus and we finally listen, really listen — until we cry out from our little faith, "Lord, help my unbelief." Help us believe, Lord, really believe, for then we will pray — really pray. And then we will listen — really listen. Lord, Beloved Son of God, be patient with us in our faithless generation, for we have strayed like sheep from the fold. Come to us in the shadow cast by Your glory until we see You — until our eyes adjust to the brilliance of the True Light and we can really see that the Kingdom and power of God have come to us; linger near until we hear, really hear — and obey.

Drive out the mute and deaf spirit within us and free us to live in the reality of the reign of God day in and day out. Amen.

# Mark 9:33-50

*Read carefully and prayerfully.* Reflect on the truth that speaks most clearly to you. Pray your own prayer in response to the Word of the Spirit to you. Offer the following prayer if it helps you express your thoughts to the Lord.

## Prayer of Response

Lord, we come in silence before You because we are ashamed to admit, even to ourselves, that we think about our "greatness" — or lack of it. We are concerned with where we stand in the opinions of others. We want to stand out, to make a difference — to leave a good and memorable mark on our sphere of life. We want to be known for what we perceive as positive achievements, though we may choose negative actions. We want to accomplish things for which we will be praised, though we disappoint others and ourselves frequently. We don't want to hear about being last and being a servant. We want to be first, at the front of the line, on top, ahead of the game.

We don't want to be relegated to what others devalue as low or dirty. We think we have skills for greater work. We think our time and contributions are more worthy than that. Besides, we want exclusive authority under Your name — certainly not to be in a position of need or helplessness. So, it is jarring to be reminded that we are actually living on the edge of hell. We are in danger of putting the wrong things forth as our priorities — of preserving our misguided means of fulfillment and of teaching this self-focused life to our children and grandchildren by example that belies our words.

What we do with our hands really matters. Where we go with our feet matters. What we look at matters. What we choose to hear matters. We should take whatever drastic steps are needed to avoid the unquenchable, fiery regrets and painful sorrows of missing Your Kingdom by living in our self-made enclaves of self-seeking prestige and influence. Lord, we have lost our fear of hell and we don't want to make sacrifices. We are softies. Wimps. And we have covered our soul hunger with that which does not satisfy. We do not long for or savor what we should.

Restore our taste for what will really nourish and fulfill our God-given longings. Season our souls with what is good and true — what will bring peace rather than judgment, joy rather than sorrow, fulfillment rather than loss, grace rather than regret. Amen.

# Mark 10:1-31

*Read carefully and prayerfully.* Reflect on the truth that speaks most clearly to you. Pray your own prayer in response to the Word of the Spirit to you. Offer the following prayer if it helps you express your thoughts to the Lord.

## Prayer of Response

Lord, I see! Everything belongs. Everything matters. Every area of life has been covered under Your authority and in Your teachings. But, there are wide discrepancies in interpretations. As scripture reveals, You reinforced the view of creation that God established family in the context of the way we are created and as a foundation of human life. In our culture, families take many shapes and expressions — and seek Your blessing. You have honored marriage and declared that adultery, fornication, and divorce are aberrations of Your intent for the union of man and woman. Surely that is the standard for all variations of family.

Yet in our human frailties, a lasting marriage commitment is a lost goal for many. There are many blessed families who rejoice in Your abounding love; yet, many more remain hurt in their fractured homes and lives. You set the example for us, setting children forth to be cherished and enabled to grow into Your image in the Kingdom of God. Yet, many are devalued. Many are struggling in the confusion, pain, and suffering of abuse, neglect, and poor training. We hurt for them and wonder how to help.

The entirety of our lives belongs under Your authority, but we get off track and need Your guidance for the next right steps. According to Your teachings, we miss the mark, sometimes by miles. You have called us — no, directed and warned us — that we must relate to You as Your children if we are to know You. Take us into Your arms, Lord Jesus. Bless us, lay Your hands upon our heads and imbue us with the power of Your indestructible life. Help us look into the words of scripture and commandments to find Your Purpose that is above the world's values, philosophies, political struggles, and treasures.

Remind us, over and over, until we get it: materialism is not Your call. What we can buy and sell is not what You value and not what will ultimately fulfill our lives. Convince us that what is right with You may be wrong with the world. Lord, we are helpless to extricate ourselves from all that we have allowed to hinder us and bind us. We have played games with You, deceiving ourselves with pretense and presumption, hoping to receive

Your grace while denying Your authority and righteous judgment. We try to push our way into the Kingdom, determined to carry along everything we decide to value, trying to force You to change Your values to ours.

Forgive us, Lord. Help us to let go of what we must in order to have what we most need for all time and eternity. We don't want to go away sorrowful, entrapped by our desires and possessions. Do the impossible for us and help us to be first at the gate with empty hands, open hearts, and willing spirits—at any and all costs. Amen.

# Mark 10:32-52

*Read carefully and prayerfully.* Reflect on the truth that speaks most clearly to you. Pray your own prayer in response to the Word of the Spirit to you. Offer the following prayer if it helps you express your thoughts to the Lord.

## Prayer of Response

Lord, stop and call for us, for we are calling out for You, crying out in sorrow, fear, and pain — even anger. When You ask, "what do You want me to do for You?" — our lists are long. Help us, like Blind Bartimaeus, to zero in on the main thing we need to seek. Help us receive our spiritual sight so that we may see clearly who You are and who we are. Jesus, Son of David, have mercy on us. Help us throw off all hindrances to faith, and to truly believe and follow You on the way to complete understanding.

Lord, You asked that same question of James and John — "What do You want me to do for You?" They wanted glory with You. Like them, we often don't know what would be entailed if we received our desires. We don't know ourselves and we don't know You as You are — only as we have been conditioned to think You are. We mistake wrong values for right values. We want power, authority, prestige, and glory. You have all that, but channel it into loving service.

You came to serve and we come to be served. Forgive us for our self-focused prayers and ambitions. Thank You, Lord, for serving us in our greatest need. Help us set forth Your greatest gift as our greatest value — that You have given Your life as a ransom for us. We were, and are, in bondage to our desires and worldly values. Nothing could ever atone for the ugliness and perversion of our souls except the purity of Your indestructible life given to cover our transgressions.

Through our faith, make our sin-sick souls well, that we may go on our way as living examples of the good news that Jesus Christ still saves, really saves, and only saves. Amen.

# Mark 11:1-21

*Read carefully and prayerfully.* Reflect on the truth that speaks most clearly to you. Pray your own prayer in response to the Word of the Spirit to you. Offer the following prayer if it helps you express your thoughts to the Lord.

## Prayer of Response

Lord, I want to be obedient — like the disciples who followed Your explicit instructions to provide a donkey for You to ride; like the villagers who responded and cooperated with Your request through Your messengers; and like the unbroken colt that accepted the weight of Your body and the direction of Your bidding. Lord, I want to praise You with unencumbered joy like those who prepared Your path with robes and leafy branches. And I want to understand You: the One who commands and sends, observes and purges, teaches indisputable truth, and imbues us with the power of forgiveness.

You hold what I need and *all* that I need: strength through faith, forgiveness for failure, and wisdom in life. Lord, I want to respond to Your authority with unquestioning obedience, with purity in worship, with priority in prayer, faith over doubt, forgiveness for all, and honesty within.

May the end result be a fruitful life in Your sight. Amen.

# Mark 11:22-33

*Read carefully and prayerfully.* Reflect on the truth that speaks most clearly to you. Pray your own prayer in response to the Word of the Spirit to you. Offer the following prayer if it helps you express your thoughts to the Lord.

## Prayer of Response

Lord, we know that we cannot play games with You. You know all our motives and see through our deceptions; You know that we are afraid of bucking the norms in our culture. We're always analyzing, weighing, and covering, even when faced with true reality. It's hard to recognize truth because the false is cloaked in convincing "authority." We are easily swayed by confident voices telling us what we want to believe. Help us pay attention to the fig trees in our lives — to the reality of what You bless and do not bless. Help us come out from behind our screens and barriers and trust You in the open.

Point out to us where we are letting doubt keep us in bondage to the very things we are praying to overcome. Help us to get in tune with our true thoughts and to deny fear of any degree. Let confidence in Your love and power overtake our questions and commitments to worldly, godless thoughts. With forgiveness at the core, teach us how to let faith reign in all of our praying and day-to-day living.

Help us trust You without questioning. Help us forsake any inclination that is based on fear or doubt. Lord Jesus Christ, help us truly have faith in God completely, without reservation. It is scary to let go of our intellectual reasoning, to trust simply and fully. Hold us steady, Lord, as we take our faltering steps into Your sovereign reign. Amen.

# Mark 12

*Read carefully and prayerfully.* Reflect on the truth that speaks most clearly to you. Pray your own prayer in response to the Word of the Spirit to you. Offer the following prayer if it helps you express your thoughts to the Lord.

## Prayer of Response

O Lord, God of the Living, it occurs to me that reading scripture is like opening a matryoshka doll. There are stories nesting inside stories and meaning inside meaning. Mark's gospel is particularly stacked with essential truths. Perhaps the inmost and central nugget of wisdom is verse 24, where Jesus pinpoints the critical issue as not knowing scripture and the power of God. Being ignorant of either is to be bereft of both. To know the power of God makes it possible to rightly discern the scriptures. To know the scriptures opens one to the power of God.

Lord, we get it. To know the power of God as we read scripture is to read with awareness of Your sovereignty and intimacy — transcendence and immanence. It is to learn with Moses, walk with Abraham, feel with Isaac, and grow in obedience with Jacob. It is to stumble and be forgiven with Peter, to be blinded with head-spinning change of perspective with Paul, and to be immersed in amazing love with John. And it is to recognize the work of God in his servants and in His Son — and to look with faith and pure allegiance to Him as the One True God. It is to recognize Your divine, ultimate, righteous authority, and to live with humility before You. It is to tend Your vineyard and to bring forth fruit pleasing to You. It is to treat Your people with honor and respect.

It is to see ourselves and to be warned of Your power, authority, and right of judgment over all. You see through our hypocrisy to the real issues, and Your teachings expose our untrue, self-serving motives. You reveal ideals that we would scorn when at our worst and overlook at our best. Lord, we don't want to be far from the Kingdom of God, or even *close* to the Kingdom. We want to be IN Your Kingdom — securely and certainly *within* — accepted and approved like the poor widow You commended for giving all she had.

We confess we are more often quibbling over earnings and possessions rather than sharing. This verse reminds us that You see us and know us through and through. You know what we give and what we withhold. You know what we share and what we hide. We are exposed and dismayed.

We know that we are far from where we need to be and we call out to be rescued from ourselves, and from the culture that ensnares us. Help us to truly render unto You, O God, all that is Yours — and to live in awareness that there is nothing that is really ours.

We pray in order to give God what is God's — our very lives. Amen.

# Mark 13

*Read carefully and prayerfully.* Reflect on the truth that speaks most clearly to you. Pray your own prayer in response to the Word of the Spirit to you. Offer the following prayer if it helps you express your thoughts to the Lord.

## Prayer of Response

Lord, this passage truly puts us on watch. It clears our perspective to understand that, while we are on an eternal journey, our pilgrimage is in the midst of passing, impermanent things. All that claims our time and energy in the world is transient and temporary. What we need is faith — to watch and to endure the death throes of a dying world system. Help us remember, as the world and its pseudo-powers thrash and clamor, that Your glorious reign is coming into view. So this dire forecast is not only of the end, but these foreboding signs are the birth pangs of Your new creation.

Help us understand that life for all time is best lived in faithfulness and reliance on the Holy Spirit. Keep us mindful that we are not alone; Your Spirit is within, ever ready to speak the truth in us, to us, and through us. Lord, we want to be faithful to Your admonition, "do not be alarmed." Keep us focused beyond the upheaval, the hatred, the terror, the struggles and confrontations, to Your glorious righteousness and lasting peace.

May our eyes see and our souls exult in Your coming with the greatest of all power and glory. Through the darkness and the shaking of all earthly powers and constraints, help us disbelieve false rumors that others believe — and help us believe the truth that others reject. Lord, we are standing on tiptoe, training our vision to discern the evidence that You are at the very gates — very near, ever watching, waiting, encouraging, and holding all things together. Help us hold on to Your words that never pass away, so that we will not be swept away in anxious foreboding and careless ignorance. Remember our frailties, O Lord, and strengthen us for Your glory and our salvation. Amen.

# Mark 14

*Read carefully and prayerfully.* Reflect on the truth that speaks most clearly to you. Pray your own prayer in response to the Word of the Spirit to you. Offer the following prayer if it helps you express your thoughts to the Lord.

## Prayer of Response

Lord, we see it. Fear and pride are our real enemies. The chief priests and scribes feared the loss of all in which they took pride for themselves. They were concerned about their lofty reputations being discredited and their perceived positions of authority being challenged. Egoism possessed them and blinded their eyes to the truth before them. The disciples, too, were unable to see clearly, so they discounted the gift of anointing being given to Jesus. They twisted an expression of pure love and gratitude into a wasteful, misplaced deed of ignorance. How like them we often are.

Though the evidence is right before our eyes, we overlook it. We become trapped in our own minds, distracted by our plans and goals; we abort our highest commitments by trying to force life to go in the direction we determine it should. Forgive the Judas in each one of us. Forgive us for dipping our bread in the bowl of Grace while living in duplicity of mind and spirit. Bring us together, Lord, to see only You: God who came in flesh, whose blood was shed at the hands of Your own created beings. You, who drank the cup of man's wrath, turned it into atonement and deliverance from the wrath we fear from God, the wrath that we fear we have earned.

We are taught that our sins of pride and prejudice deserve only death and hellish outcomes. Yet, You have given us a cup of unending love to drink — a cup of unimaginable Grace. Like Peter, we break down and weep when we recognize our shortsightedness and lack of commitment to the One whose blood was poured out in our behalf. Like Peter, we are amazed that You love us so much that nothing can eternally separate us from You, Our Beloved Savior, Good Shepherd, and Divine Friend.

Thank You that Your redemption does not fade away, but is ever ready for any and all who return to the garden of holy love. Here I am, Lord, ready to watch and pray so that I will no longer run away, no longer betray and deny, no longer bluff and brag, no longer blame and shame, no longer fear and forsake. I return, Lord, with my flask of anointing oil to anoint You as Master and Lord, Redeemer and Healer, Wonderful Counselor, Mighty God, Everlasting Father, Prince of Peace. Amen.

# Mark 15

*Read carefully and prayerfully.* Reflect on the truth that speaks most clearly to you. Pray your own prayer in response to the Word of the Spirit to you. Offer the following prayer if it helps you express your thoughts to the Lord.

## Prayer of Response

Lord, we stand wordless before the cross, aghast at the horror of it all. We weep with the women who followed You and ministered to You, who were left forlorn, watching their merciful, wise teacher, healer, and prophet doomed and helplessly tortured upon a cross. We wonder whether Barabbas was watching — whether he had any idea that Jesus' death had set him free. Did he care? How many like him have missed the personal meaning of it all? How much do we miss?

From all directions came mocking accusations and declarations — that You were the King of the Jews or a blasphemous traitor — from Jews who wanted deliverance from Rome, from religious leaders who denied Your power and right to the title Messiah, from Pilate and the soldiers who were amused or annoyed at the absurdities, from disciples who knew Your true authority and were bewildered by Your submission to what they thought You could defeat.

Would we have proclaimed You as truly King, or joined with the scoffers? Do we now? Would we have had to be forced at sword point to take the weight of the cross, or would we have rushed forward to help, recognizing that we deserve it far more than You? Would we have watched in curiosity or dread as the tragic pathos unfolded before us, as soldiers crucified the wonder-working rabbi and carelessly cast lots for his plain clothing? I imagine I would have been overwhelmed with fear and horror as I sought to make sense of the trapped and dying man on the cross, who just days before had taught, blessed, healed, and even raised the dead. Yet there He was — dying, able to save others but not saving himself.

I choose the only explanation that makes sense — that You truly could not save Yourself if You were to truly save others. For we didn't need healing just from our diseases and distorted lives, we needed rescue from the wages of death that our sin has earned us. But first we need to recognize that we truly have sinned and stand guilty before a Holy God, unfit to enter His righteous presence. Why is that so hard for us to do? It's not like we would be standing with the minority!

As the Prophet Isaiah said, our sins have separated us from God (Isaiah 59:2). We sense the distance and the disparity, and we cry out in our need: Lord Jesus, save us, for surely You are the Son of God. Amen.

# Mark 15 continued

*Read carefully and prayerfully.* Reflect on the truth that speaks most clearly to you. Pray your own prayer in response to the Word of the Spirit to you. Offer the following prayer if it helps you express your thoughts to the Lord.

## Prayer of Response

We are reminded that the prophet Isaiah declared, "Behold, the Lord's hand is not shortened, that it cannot save, or His ear dull that it cannot hear; but your iniquities have made a separation between you and your God, and your sins have hid his face from you so that he does not hear" (Isaiah 59:1-2). Wow. Lord, have You heard and kept record of all my murmurings and complaining, even the small slights and offenses? I am undone, helpless to rectify the mounting truth.

Are You pointing to the times I could have helped and supported someone — but took care of personal urgencies and desires instead? Do You mean the times I stood and sang the hymns of commitment and essentially "lied"? I obviously did not really mean "Have Thine Own Way." Did I? I surely didn't follow through with "I Surrender All." Did I? I sang "What a Friend We Have in Jesus," but sat mute when I could have shared Your friendship with the friendless who were uncomfortably different from me.

Lord, we see a paradox. The scriptures assert, "the wages of sin is death" (Romans 6:23). The biblical records also declare that You, O Jesus, were completely without sin (2 Corinthians 5:21 NIV). So, if death is our human lot because of sin, You could not die. Yet, You died. You participated in our humanity — but not in our sin. And, still, You died. It follows that surely it is as scripture declares: our sins were transferred, placed upon Your head in the crown of thorns, across Your back in the blows of the clawed whips, nailed into Your hands and feet, and atoned for in the blood that flowed along the Via Dolorosa and down the rough wood of the cross. We declare with New Testament authors, "Behold, the Lamb of God . . . slain from the foundation of the world," who takes away our sins (John 1:29; Revelation 13:8 KJV). It is a mystery. It is the great gift. It is Grace.

For the sin-sick soul, there is atonement. As You said, O Lord, those who are well may not personally feel a need for such a sacrifice-bought redemption. They may not be riddled with guilt, though they may be comforted that You have provided "at-one-ment"; but for the sin-sick soul, full atonement is the only thing that rings true — that makes sense — that convinces them that they can truly be justified before God. I am among them, O Lord, needing convincing evidence. Atonement proves redemption belongs to me as well. Praise God from Whom all blessings flow.

We join the centurion in proclaiming, "Truly, this man was the Son of God!" — and IS the Son of God, Redeemer, Resurrected Lord — my King. Amen and Amen.

# Mark 16

*Read carefully and prayerfully.* Reflect on the truth that speaks most clearly to you. Pray your own prayer in response to the Word of the Spirit to you. Offer the following if it helps you express your thoughts to the Lord.

## Prayer of Response

Lord, we can't help but be amazed: an empty tomb, an angel in the tomb, empty grave cloths, missing body, instructions to tell others the unbelievable, puzzling, and terrifying news. No wonder the women ran in trembling astonishment. No wonder they said nothing at first. Who would believe emotional women? Who would believe such an outlandish account?

As the unusual occurrences mounted, so did the recollections and insight, until they "got it." So it is with us; we hear the gospel, reflect on it personally, and then one day it clicks and we know that we have been in communion with You. You appear to us in "another form" as well, so that we can join the saints who have discerned Your presence by faith. Without faith, all the occurrences could be denied, dismissed, even explained. Reason explains. Faith sees, believes, knows. Faith is the way You have chosen for us to enter into Your realm and to welcome You as a real presence in our realm, where we deal with demons, deadly dangers, and diseases.

Thank You that our greatest fears fall impotent when we welcome You by faith. We know that there is nothing to fear. This life is a part of an eternal mystery that is undisturbed by the worst of our experiences. Forgive us for our unbelief and hardness of heart, which deny the power and essence of the signs of Your presence. We deny the signs and they dissipate. We honor them and they surface. We let our intellect pull the shades down so we cannot truly see Your glory. In denying the signs of Your presence, we essentially deny Your resurrection. When we deny Your resurrection, we deny our eternal life. And we are left bewildered and bereft at any tomb — and terrified before the gaping hole of our own tomb-to-be.

Lord, pull up the shades of our intellectual misgivings and help us to see the signs of Your indestructible life at work to save those who believe and live in communion with You. May we be so convinced and motivated by faith that we will proclaim the amazing gospel wherever we are, with the power of Your Spirit confirming the Truth at work in us and for us. Help us move boldly against negative voices and actions.

May our faith save us, and others, from the condemnation of unbelief that barricades us from Your active, loving presence and power. Amen.

# Praying Through Luke

## Luke 1:1-38

*Read carefully and prayerfully.* Reflect on the truth that speaks most clearly to you. Pray your own prayer in response to the Word of the Spirit to you. Offer the following prayer if it helps you express your thoughts to the Lord.

### Prayer of Response

Lord, it means so much to hold in our hands this ancient document of historical record — an orderly account — that has been carefully researched by one who followed closely the experiences and accomplishments of the early disciples. I am so grateful to be a recipient of this knowledge from someone who lived and moved among the "eyewitnesses and ministers of the word." What a gift to have this precious narrative so that I may know the truth of what happened and what it means — that "word" of life which unfolded in Jesus the Christ.

We come to this "word" like either Zechariah or Mary. Either we ignore the validity of what is revealed to us, and so persist with our questions of disbelief; or we gladly and reverently welcome the mystery, committing our lives to the new life that comes to us through Your Spirit. Both Zechariah and Mary were "righteous, walking in all the commandments and ordinances of the Lord blameless," but they responded to the wonder differently. We are humbled along with Zechariah by the discipline of muteness. Like him, we cannot imagine our lives any different, though we long for more awareness of the divine in the everyday corners of our lives.

We are left speechless by our unbelief — our intellectual reservations — and the gospel is stymied and hampered for us by our doubt-filled reticence.

Help Thou our unbelief. Help us believe the good news that You will come to us; that the Holy Spirit will come upon us; the power of the Most High will overshadow us; the life of Christ will shape us into the image that was intended for our souls; and we shall each know ourselves to be a child of God.

It seems too good to be true. Help us dispel the question of "how can I know this is true?" We have Luke's well-researched and carefully completed account. Gabriel himself has been sent from God to ensure that we have the good news. So, the only way forward into this new reality is in the attitude of Mary. Lord, behold I am Your child and willing to serve You with all humility from this moment forward. Let it be to me according to Your Word. Accomplish the impossible while we watch with the wondering eyes and grateful hearts of children who have not yet had the world reduced to reasoned speculations and rationalizations.

Son of the Most High, reign over our fears and failures, our achievements and successes. Reign supreme, O Lord God Our Maker and Deliverer. Reign forever without end. Amen.

# Luke 1:39-66

*Read carefully and prayerfully.* Reflect on the truth that speaks most clearly to you. Pray your own prayer in response to the Word of the Spirit to you. Offer the following prayer if it helps you express your thoughts to the Lord.

## Prayer of Response

Lord, when Your Word comes to us with personal significance, we receive energy to hasten into all that You have promised. Lead us to the people who know You, love You, and who will welcome us with joy into the community of growing faith. Sad to say, many do not find deep spiritual community, even within our churches. We long for the kind of joy experienced by Mary, Elizabeth, and the babe in Elizabeth's womb. Help us believe with that same excitement and deep assurance that there will be fulfillment of what has been told to us through the Word of Your Spirit in our day.

May our souls be unleashed to recognize the rare truth of Your personal involvement in our lives. May our faith burst forth to magnify Your name and to rejoice in You, O God our Savior, who pays attention to the low estate of Your children. You, who are Mighty God, have come to us and done great things for us. Holy is Your name. We are touched by Your mercy that has poured into generation after generation of human experience. We look to You for the deliverance we need in our day. Show forth Your strength to the nations. Bring down and scatter those who are prideful in their imaginations and who bring misery on those of low degree.

Fill the hungry with good things and send the prideful rich away to learn humility and compassion so that they will not need to go sadly away from You. In remembrance of Your help to people of ages past, reach out to us with Your mighty arm and gather us into the circle of Your divine love. Show us our capacity to receive Your Spirit and to become a channel for Your grace to those who live in fear and without hope. And help us turn to our families, neighbors, and kinsfolk with the assurance, conviction, and commitment to honor Your Word.

Praise be to You, O Lord, for You have come and have redeemed Your people. Amen.

# Luke 1:67-80

*Read carefully and prayerfully.* Reflect on the truth that speaks most clearly to you. Pray your own prayer in response to the Word of the Spirit to you. Offer the following prayer if it helps you express your thoughts to the Lord.

## Prayer of Response

Lord, thank You for giving us something to hold on to: a horn of salvation, such as was figuratively built into the altar of the tabernacle (Exodus 27:1-2). Like Joab clung to the horns of the tabernacle altar when he feared for his life, so we cling to Your promises as we encounter the fearful times in our lives — times when we have given allegiance to the wrong voices, acted arrogantly, dishonored Your mercy, and encountered the hateful spirits among people with whom we must interact (1 Kings 2:28). We cling, Lord, to You — to Your grace and mercy — to Your love — and to Your power to deliver us and set our feet on even ground again.

The ground under us is slippery — wet with the blood and tears of all those who have felt hated and mistreated. It's not just our tears from our own grief. It's not just our blood from injustices inflicted upon us by others. It's the tears and blood of those we have injured and grieved by our careless oversights, apathy, and reluctance to confront evil. We have been too busy and too comfortable to rescue or comfort others. But, here we cling to the horn of salvation by faith and plead for the mercy promised to the people of faith in all generations.

We plead for that which we do not deserve because we believe You have visited and redeemed Your people who have failed. We are among those who need Your mercy, Lord. Remember Your Holy Covenant to all people, and forgive us through Your tender mercy. Increase our knowledge and understanding of Your salvation, which shines like light into our darkness. Dispel the shadows of fear, deliver us from all that binds us in prideful sin, and guide us to serve You with assurance in holy and righteous living all the days of our lives.

Guide our feet into the way of peace and salvation for all. Help us grow and become strong, filling all the corners of our minds with Your Holy Spirit. Dispel the shadows and shine forth in glory, O Lord God of Israel and of All. Help the rescued to become rescuers, O God our Deliverer. Amen.

# Luke 2:1-21

*Read carefully and prayerfully.* Reflect on the truth that speaks most clearly to you. Pray your own prayer in response to the Word of the Spirit to you. Offer the following prayer if it helps you express your thoughts to the Lord.

## Prayer of Response

Lord, we keep all these things and ponder them in our hearts. Like Mary, there is no way to fully comprehend experiences that occur outside our understanding of what is real and normal. We understand taxes and decrees, census and government authority, disruption and upheaval, travel and crowds. Our hearts are touched by the pathos of this couple, misunderstood by many, forced to travel during pregnancy and to seek lodging far from home in a strange town, to no avail. We are dismayed that they must live in a stable, but horrified when a baby has to be born in such a place and laid in a feeding trough for a cradle. But, we understand the reality.

What we don't comprehend is "the glory of the Lord" that shone around the shepherds who were first to hear the astounding news. We, too, would be frightened by light originating from no source that we know — no lantern, no sun, no moon, no star — just there — shining in the dark night. We don't understand the appearance of an angel—a presence, a being of intelligence and discernible speech, speaking in the language of Mary and Joseph — a presence not of human origin. And we can barely imagine an entire host of such angels singing praises to God.

We understand how and why the shepherds were filled — overwhelmed — with fear. When we can't explain, we fear and we marvel. While others may continue to wonder, doubt, or dismiss, we believe what we have "heard and seen" as it has been told to us in this beloved story. We join with the shepherds to glorify and praise God for the good news of great joy: that a Savior has come to all the people — a Savior who is Christ the Lord.

It is too unbelievable not to be true. It is too needed not to be true. We need a Savior. Oh, how much we need a Savior. Praise God from Whom all blessings flow. We HAVE a Savior and His Name is Jesus. Come, Lord Jesus, save us from ourselves and from the worldly influences that keep us from being the holy and righteous people You want us to be — on earth, in real time, in flesh, blood, and soul.

Glory to God in the highest! On earth, grant peace to all who seek Your favor. Amen.

# Luke 2:21-51

*Read carefully and prayerfully.* Reflect on the truth that speaks most clearly to you. Pray your own prayer in response to the Word of the Spirit to you. Offer the following prayer if it helps you express your thoughts to the Lord.

## Prayer of Response

Lord Jesus, Son of God and Son of Man, Your earthly manifestation amazes us, for You are ordinary in extra-ordinary ways and extra-ordinary in ordinary ways. Your humanity obscures Your divinity and Your divinity reveals Your humanity. This passage opens a window on Your boyhood, family customs, and connections, on Mary and Joseph's admirable sense of parental authority and responsibility, on Your personable character, the expanse of Your understanding, and the depth of Your soul. You were deep in God and lived in a family that was deep in God-honoring customs. And You were obedient. You lived as we know we should and as we wish we had all our lives.

Here we have a snapshot of a few instances in Your earthly life, and we want to learn from these brief scenarios. Lord, help us be faithful to customs that shape us in righteousness, as You were. Help us hold back from time to time from the delight of interaction with kinsfolk and acquaintances in order to expand our knowledge of You. Bring us under the work of Your Holy Spirit, so we may recognize where You are in our lives. Draw us aside from the crowd to be still in order to know God more fully. We want to be teachable as You were in Your life with God.

May our eyes see Thy salvation for all people more clearly and reveal the light of Your glory as we grow in faith. Lord, help us focus on You with more and more intent until it can be said of us that we honor God night and day.

Lord, we look to You for consolation and redemption, for all our certain hope springs only from You. Help us to obey Your leading and to increase in wisdom. Fill our years with meaningful days, and help us grow in favor with You and Your people. Guide us in a world where the sign of the cross is scorned, or trivialized into a sentimental symbol, rather than revered for the redemption and healing that it brings.

May the thoughts of our hearts reveal our abiding thankfulness for Your gracious entrance into our world and our lives. Amen.

# Luke 3

*Read carefully and prayerfully.* Reflect on the truth that speaks most clearly to you. Pray your own prayer in response to the Word of the Spirit to you. Offer the following prayer if it helps you express your thoughts to the Lord.

## Prayer of Response

Lord, this passage is full of names. You never forget a name. Every person's life is remembered — blessed — and judged. We don't like to think about the judgment. It frightens us. It discourages us. Maybe it even angers us. Many refuse to hold it to be a true reality, but Luke called it good news (vv. 17-18), and then told about Herod's evil. It IS good news that evil like Herod's is not accepted in Your Kingdom. And it is good news that repentance opens the door, even for a Herod, to leave evil behind, so that he may enter in through repentance and faith.

When we recognize the barriers we have raised in relationships and with God, it is good news that the mountain of guilt can be brought down. It is good news that the crooked, deceitful ways can be straightened. It is good news that the rough, callous, uncaring words can be replaced with smooth, healing words. It is good news that we can be baptized: washed and renewed through the love of the Holy Spirit.

It is good news that evil will not last, but will be removed like useless chaff. It is good news that Jesus brings the cleansing of baptism and the fire of judgment. How could salvation be otherwise? Salvation is deliverance from something — from evil that needs to be left behind and ended, burned away and washed away. That is good news — that evil will end. It will not abide always. And we kindle the fire for its destruction every time we recognize it for what it is and turn away from it. When we recognize and meet the needs of others, we judge the evil of selfishness and it shrivels. When we refuse actions that help us but defraud others, we name evil for what it is and burn it like chaff.

Lord, thank You for looking past all the prestige that blinds us, and for choosing an unknown man out of the wilderness who could see clearly and proclaim certainly that we need to change. And thank You that John's message assures us of what we need most: forgiveness of sins. We do sin. There is still such a thing as sin. In spite of the denial of our culture, we do all sin; and sin matters to You. In today's world, many sin very badly. We admit it and we want to be separated from the chaff of sin in our lives.

We want the regrets to burn away and the good fruits to begin to grow. Lord, what shall we do? Help us repent — truly turn away from all our crooked, prideful, callous ways. Forgive our selfish, evil ways. Yes, help us see and name our own evil for what it is. Deliver us from it, for Thine is the Kingdom, the Power and the Glory forever. Amen.

# Luke 4

*Read carefully and prayerfully.* Reflect on the truth that speaks most clearly to you. Pray your own prayer in response to the Word of the Spirit to you. Offer the following prayer if it helps you express your thoughts to the Lord.

## Prayer of Response

Here, Lord, we see You — led by the Spirit and tempted by the devil — and left hungry. We understand. It is the ongoing environment of our lives. But we settle into duplicity, while Your resolute commitment to honor God's purpose never wavered. We waver. You did not allow Your human nature to rule, but made it serve God. We are self-serving and we bend easily to cultural and personal pressures. We blame our human frailties. But, You were completely human, so You would have shared those human frailties. Yet You refused to use Your power of indestructible Life for selfish purposes. You remained human and unselfish. You call and empower us to do the same.

You appealed always to God's higher authority and refused to make a spectacle out of worship and faith. We submit to lesser authority. We applaud spectacles. You trusted God and stood firm against a bargain with Him. We propose alternatives. You said on the eve of the crucifixion, "As the Father hath sent me, even so send I You" (John 10:21). Us, Lord? Me? Sent as You are sent? I certainly would have to say that I am light years from Your capacity for righteousness. Or am I? I'm fully human. You are fully human. So, being human is not an excuse for sin. Then I need to step up to my full capacity of humanity — for righteousness.

Help me. Help us. Help us become more and more willing and more and more committed — more fully resolved to honor God in all things as You do. Help us hear and follow our marching orders in Your call and mission: to preach good news to the poor in spirit, for indeed we do have good news. It is good news that we, too, can withstand evil. There is good news for those afflicted and oppressed in their lives and their souls. Help us proclaim Your freedom of conscience to all who are held captive by social, cultural, religious, and political ideologies. Help us open the eyes that are blinded by this world's glitz and glamour — let them see it's all a sham blocking the view of Your true glorious reality.

Help us set people free through words and deeds of faith, hope, and love. May Your gracious words and pure example always draw out our wonder, praise — and devotion. Lean over us, lay Your hands upon us, and rebuke the demonic influences and desires that lie to us, confuse us, restrict us and corrupt us. Heal us, too, of all our diseases of mind, body and spirit.

Stay near us, Lord Jesus, and prepare us to go with You in helping others. Empower us to overcome ourselves and to serve You for the good of others, in the power of the Spirit. Amen.

# Luke 5:1-32

*Read carefully and prayerfully.* Reflect on the truth that speaks most clearly to you. Pray your own prayer in response to the Word of the Spirit to you. Offer the following prayer if it helps you express your thoughts to the Lord.

## Prayer of Response

Lord, here our faith is ignited. Combustible hope springs into the fire of faith with this kindling. We press toward You to hear the Word of God that You expressed, revealed, and embodied. At Your Word, Lord, we will push out into the deep and work and wait for a catch. We want to learn like Simon Peter that Your knowledge and wisdom are omnipotent. When we fully get that as he did, we too will be dismayed at how unworthy we are in Your presence. We are so far from Your ways — so different, so selfish, so faithless, so ignorant, so disobedient, so unbelieving, so unfruitful — and so unfinished.

You know that, and still You say, "Do not be afraid." Thank You, Lord, for that — for Your kindness, understanding, compassion, and mercy. That is why we follow, leaving everything that prevents our following. We are afraid and we are relieved that You care about us even in our failures. That is why we come to You with our dis-ease and our diseases. We hope, when we reach out to You with faith in Your power and compassion to heal, that You will touch us with healing grace and give assurance that Your yearning will is our wholeness.

Help, Lord, our fearful, wavering faith — our underlying unbelief — for we mourn our loss of wholeness. We grieve for all those reaching out and finding no cure. We blush for paying attention to those who make a circus-like spectacle of faith for healing when the sick are not better. But, we do want healing and are puzzled when it doesn't come. Great multitudes gathered in Your day to hear Your teaching because they ultimately wanted healing more than understanding. And You withdrew to pray. While people waited, longing for health, You withdrew to pray. So, we follow. We pray and wait and wonder. There is much to understand.

We are paralyzed by grief and fear, burying our loved ones and lying helpless before You in our sickness and sadness. Forgive our doubt, calm our fear, correct our error, and break the power that binds us in sickness of mind, soul, and body. Set us free. We repent of our self-assertion. In Your time and in the way of highest good, heal us, O Great Physician. Open our understanding to right expectations, O Lord. Let us see, know, and tell of amazing acts of grace in our day that will cause hearts to sing with glorious praise for Your mighty works of authority and grace.

"Mercy drops round us are falling, but for the showers we plead."[2] A tiny spark of faith has flashed; fan it into full flame, O Lord. We wait, O Lord. Amen.

# Luke 5:33-39

*Read carefully and prayerfully.* Reflect on the truth that speaks most clearly to you. Pray your own prayer in response to the Word of the Spirit to you. Offer the following prayer if it helps you express your thoughts to the Lord.

## Prayer of Response

Lord, what we need is to be near You. Mourning ceased and fasting was unnecessary when the disciples were with You. They were like wedding guests caught up in the joy and plenty of the occasion. When we pull away, the joy diminishes, even ceases. When we are far away, we must fast until we remember we are the ones who moved away.

You are where You always are: nearer than our nearest breath, though barricaded by our unrighteousness. We try to patch things up, but Your new ways and our old ways don't match. They don't adhere to one another. Our lives are dry and brittle, incapable of holding Your Spirit. We stretch out to You seeking restoration of mind, heart, soul, and body. We need to be filled to the brim with Your Spirit, flushing out the old and infusing us with the new. But first we need to be *made* new — again. We need to draw back into Your warm womb of grace and be reshaped according to Your likeness. Like clay on the potter's wheel, we need to be remolded into a vessel fit to hold Your Spirit.

Help us give up our arguing and clamoring over rules and regulations and all that will pass away with time. Help us to look past all of that so we may see that Your love precedes and trumps law, that the rules we make need to be kept flexible as wineskins so that human need is met. Help us see that is Your focus, beaming toward the least and the worst around us (and in us). That is what drew people to You: Your compassion and Your indestructible life. The power of health and wholeness in Your life healed all who touched You. Lord, we want to stay close to You so that the power of Your life may be known in our inmost being — in our very bone and marrow.

We see that You spent whole nights in prayer. Help us find balance between work and prayer, recreation and prayer, selfish pursuits and prayer. Help us reorder our work, our play, and all of our endeavors so that they glorify You and serve the needs of others more than ourselves — or at least as much as ourselves. That would be a big step forward. Renew our lives so that we take hold of Your Spirit for all we think and do, to look out at the world from Your view and to see the needs within our reach.

Help us quit quibbling over what is in or out, and who is in or out. Help us to be more concerned with who You are, where we are in relation to You, and whether we are being made new by the newness of Your Spirit in all aspects of our lives. Amen.

# Luke 6:1-19

*Read carefully and prayerfully.* Reflect on the truth that speaks most clearly to you. Pray your own prayer in response to the Word of the Spirit to you. Offer the following prayer if it helps you express your thoughts to the Lord.

## Prayer of Response

Lord, help us view life through Your lens. We more often look out at others in various situations through Pharisaic lenses. We look with critical, judgmental vision. It is the way we have been shaped, sad to say, even in our churches. We learned to judge and condemn, rather than to discern and affirm. We learned to look past human need, choosing to see human fault. We put law before love when we should put love before law. Like the Pharisees of old, we miss the point.

As You said, love fulfills God's most important commandments: "Love the Lord your God with all your heart and with all your soul and with all your mind and with all your strength. . . Love your neighbor as yourself. There is no commandment greater than these" (Mark 12:29-31 NIV). Help us learn from You how to do what is good and right, practical and effective in order to meet need — to feed the hungry, even on the Sabbath. In fact, teach us how to keep the Sabbath in a spirit of love and wonder. You are worthy of a day of devotion. The world needs people dedicated to a day of doing good. We need a day to rest our weary souls in Your loving care. Most of all, we need a day to be still and to listen for Your "still, small voice," as Elijah learned to do (1 Kings 19:12).

Show us how to do good and save lives rather than hold them back by indifference or dismissal. Lord, call forth leaders in our day who will lead in love and wisdom. Call on us, Lord. We stretch out our hands to have right purpose restored. We come with unclean spirits, impure minds, damaged souls. We seek to touch Your Spirit and to know Your power. Please cleanse and heal us, restore and renew us, for Thy name's sake, in keeping with who You are — for Your glory and for our joy. Amen.

# Luke 6:20-38

*Read carefully and prayerfully.* Reflect on the truth that speaks most clearly to you. Pray your own prayer in response to the Word of the Spirit to you. Offer the following prayer if it helps you express your thoughts to the Lord.

## Prayer of Response

Thank You Lord, that You always lift up Your eyes upon us — that You watch and observe us with a caring, constant gaze. Direct Your voice to our waiting ears and our open hearts until we comprehend what You see.

Thank You that Your blessings are for all Your disciples and not only for those gifted and empowered for extraordinary leadership. Thank You that those who have little in the way of worldly goods can have a whole lot of God, even the Kingdom of God within. Thank You that those who hunger for more than mere earthly morsels will be sustained with lasting spiritual nourishment; and those who are engulfed in human sorrow will break through into joy. Thank You that You take note of the inequities of life, the baseless hatred, the unfair exclusions, and the devastating slanders. We rejoice to have this glimpse of restoration, satisfaction, fulfillment, and inclusion.

You are the Great Equalizer and heaven is the Great Equality. Lord, You turn the world upside right and it astonishes us, for we are so accustomed to, and shaped by, the attitudes of an upside down world. We don't realize that we are living upside down until You remind us. We have been blinded by the enticement of riches in funds, food, fun, and fame; we have dismissed and neglected the poor as unmotivated and derelict. We laugh at trifles when we should cry over the needs of others. We value recognition for ourselves, and feel justified by anger when our reputation is diminished by the thoughtless, selfish words or deeds of others. Sad to say, we do ourselves as much harm as our enemies when we respond with angry tirades. It is hard to hear Your call to love over of the angry clamoring in our minds and hearts about real or perceived offenses and desires. Our souls are diminished and we often have our own selves to blame.

Help me love each and every person, known and unknown, as if they were I. Better yet, help me love all people as if they were You, for You identify with each of us. Instead of judging and retaliating for, or barricading against, perceived infractions of my codes and standards, help me care about the concerns and needs covered up by selfish, demanding behavior.

Help me give what I most long to receive in merciful love, non-prejudiced generosity, and full forgiveness. Open my eyes to true blessedness in things that can't be seen but can be received in the soul.

As You give what is best, help me do the same. Amen.

# Luke 6:39-49

*Read carefully and prayerfully.* Reflect on the truth that speaks most clearly to you. Pray your own prayer in response to the Word of the Spirit to you. Offer the following prayer if it helps you express your thoughts to the Lord.

## Prayer of Response

Lord, it takes our breath away to hear the stakes laid out for us. We must lay a right foundation for our lives, or all we trust in can be washed away without a trace of lasting significance. We must dig down deep in the good soil of truth when we plant our tree of life, or we will not produce fruit that blesses anyone or that truly honors You. The right foundation is laid in full recognition of Your authority as Divine Lord — Lord of All, Lord of Truth, and Lord of Life.

In Matthew's account, we read how You said even more about Lordship (Matthew 7:21-23). You said that calling You Lord is not enough. We must live in obedience to what it means to call You Lord. Your Lordship is the Lordship of the God of Heaven, and the will of the Father is the one true foundation of authority for our lives. Everything we do in life is meaningless, if it is not done because of Your authority. The fruit of our lives will lie decaying on the ground, if we are not planted securely in Your authority and nurtured deeply in Your Spirit. Forgive me, Lord, for singing Your songs, reading Your words, serving Your church, giving tithes for Your glory — but not obeying the yearning of Your loving will.

We have sought our own way around Your way. We have doubted Your work and denied its true meaning. We have listened to a distorted gospel that sounds much like the world's philosophies. We have built a house of cards that will fall flat when the wind of Your Spirit blows in upon it. Blow, Lord Jesus, blow away our false beliefs and expose the truth to our astonished souls until we truly cry out, "Lord, Lord, what would You have us to do?" Amen.

# Luke 7

*Read carefully and prayerfully.* Reflect on the truth that speaks most clearly to you. Pray your own prayer in response to the Word of the Spirit to you. Offer the following prayer if it helps you express your thoughts to the Lord.

## Prayer of Response

Lord, we heard of Jesus a long time ago and we still marvel at the record of His life. We have heard the stories and visualized His life and wondered at it all. It is so far from our comprehension and experience. Through all the pages of scripture, we have seen the blind receive their sight, staggering at the sight of trees and their loved ones. We have beheld the lame leap with joy, take up their pallets, and walk, even run, home — proclaiming all the way that Your compassion and power healed them. We have seen the lepers fall at Your feet — emaciated, sick, and disfigured — and rise with flawless skin and restored limbs, able to go home to their friends and family, to live productively and gratefully.

We have heard the deaf rejoice at the sound of Your voice, at the voices of their loved ones, the song of birds, and at the reading of scripture in synagogues. We have seen the joyful faces of the poor who found hope through Your compassionate welcome and acceptance of all in equal measure. We have seen the hungry fed and we have witnessed the young man of Na'ir sit up on his funeral bier to greet his astonished and overwhelmed mother.

Forgive us for wanting to see such signs and wonders, but we do long to see more evidence of Your power in our times—more healing and more conversion, more joy. Help us understand the full meaning of it all, so that our expectations will be well founded. Forgive our wanderlust, our searching for substitute satisfaction in stimulating entertainment, impressive fashion, exotic experiences, affluent lifestyle, intellectual prowess, and great religious knowledge. Remind us that we have "seen and heard" all that is of true importance. God has visited His people — and never left.

You have come to us and revealed Your purpose. You have thrown Your searchlight on our souls, which were seeking need-based faith, humility, repentance, and gratitude. We stand with our alabaster jars of precious, fragrant ointment and join the woman of the streets in expressing our grateful devotion to You. You have come with the message that we need to hear and the help we need for our lives. You have brought sense to religion and You have given us the thing we most need: forgiveness. You have shown that when faith and love come together, forgiveness follows.

We come to be forgiven much, for we have failed much. We come to be saved, rescued, delivered, to renew our focus, and to accept the purpose of God in every aspect of our lives. Help us to take our place among those who take no offense in You. Guard our thoughts, words, and actions so that we will no longer darken Your name.

We don't want to miss the way, Lord, so stay close beside us, we pray. Amen.

# Luke 8

*Read carefully and prayerfully.* Reflect on the truth that speaks most clearly to you. Pray your own prayer in response to the Word of the Spirit to you. Offer the following prayer if it helps you express your thoughts to the Lord.

## Prayer of Response

Master, Master, we are perishing. It seems that You are asleep while we are buffeted by tremendous storms of life. We are afraid. We try to believe, but the seeds of truth get snatched away by scoffers, and even scholars, who declare faith to be politically incorrect, scientifically unfounded, historically inaccurate, intellectually empty, and culturally irrelevant. Few people today hold Your Word in honest and good hearts. Faith is broken into pieces, dissected, disbelieved, disregarded, and trampled under foot, rendered useless and impotent before unbelieving eyes. And it is choked by the cares and pleasures of life. We worry and fear, frantically dashing from one empty solution to another.

We fill our minds, hearts, and time with the pursuit of our goals for prosperity, control, and reputation. We seek our own comfort and pleasure at the expense of the earth and of the unseen, oppressed people who provide cheap labor, but who never reap the profits for a sustainable life. Help us bring the light of truth to the light of day. Help us cease hiding from Your divine illumination of what is good and right — and what is evil and wrong. Help us turn back to hear, really hear, Your Word and to believe it to really believe it, and to do the things that believing requires.

O Lord Jesus, the One who commands wind and water — command our souls this day. Deliver us from the pressures and influences that drive us away from You and true life. We reach out, O Lord, to touch You and be healed of our infirmities of mind, soul, and body — especially of our faithlessness. Arise and rebuke the raging waves of doubts, fears, confusion, and anxieties. Help us to believe and to go in peace. Help us bring forth the fruit of faith, patiently trusting, obeying, and sharing the good news of Your divine authority, purpose, and help.

O God, You have been our help in ages past, and we know You to be our hope for the years of our lives and for the ages to come. Help Thou our unbelief and forgive our disobedience. Help us arise to honor You day by day, all the way. Amen.

# Luke 9

*Read carefully and prayerfully.* Reflect on the truth that speaks most clearly to you. Pray your own prayer in response to the Word of the Spirit to you. Offer the following prayer if it helps you express your thoughts to the Lord.

## Prayer of Response

Lord, the crowds rush together when great things happen, but they disperse when asked to *be* great in the midst of hardship. We are in that crowd. We come to You for the healing, for the love and forgiveness, and to hear about the might and mercy of God and His Kingdom. But, when faced with options of struggle and discomfort, we look for all possible reasons not to follow. We close our doors while You open Yours.

We forbid when You welcome. We choose to depend upon ourselves and our stuff, rather than on God's care and guidance. We see that path into Your Kingdom and stare past the entrance — often shrinking back because of the uncomfortable imaginings that strike terror in our hearts. We want a place to lay our heads, with familiar faces and comforting experiences. We don't want to deal with suffering. It is not until illness, misfortune, or disease destroys our comfort zones that many of us are ready to open our hearts to You. Then many are ready to believe in You. There are also those who become angry and challenge Your place in their lives. Thank You that You see us, know us, and welcome us whenever or however we come.

Help us remember who You are — The Christ of God, the Son of the Living God — and who we are — created beings, like sheep in need of a shepherd. Help us listen to You, the Good Shepherd, above the din of voices that drown out all but theirs. We live in, and are part of, a faithless, failing, and perverse generation. Enable us to see what is real and to give up our self-importance, which forbids or diminishes the value of others. Help us deny the empty, temporal promises of all that enamors us, so that we can keep our focus on the reign of God in our lives, day by day, whatever the cost.

Lord Jesus, the voice of God instructs us to listen to You. We hear Your call to cease depending on ourselves, on what we can control, or on what others think. Help us let go by seeing what really matters. We hear You tell us to feed the hungry. Help us organize our lives differently, so that others can be fed, too. We hear You say to give up the whole world, to deny the pseudo-power of its greatness and allurements, to escape its siren calls, and all that causes us to lose our true selves, which are made in the image of God.

We have become misshapen and need to divest ourselves of all that blinds, blocks, and hinders us from living in awareness of the majesty of You, O God. Lord, we step forward to put our hand to the plow and not look back. Hold us there and guide us to plow straight rows. Amen.

# Luke 10

*Read carefully and prayerfully.* Reflect on the truth that speaks most clearly to you. Pray your own prayer in response to the Word of the Spirit to you. Offer the following prayer if it helps you express your thoughts to the Lord.

## Prayer of Response

Lord, we can hardly identify with the disciples being sent out with no provisions. It's foreign to us. Like good Boy Scouts or Girl Scouts, we have been trained to "be prepared." The very fact that we can't trust people to help us and the fact that there are "wolves" out there, is all the more reason to prepare. Help us to learn to depend on and trust in You alone, and to want nothing as much as a place in Your circle of obedient followers, laboring in the business of taking the good news to others.

The harvest is heavy and the dangers are real. Help us be people of peace who go where You send and who share peace as we go. Lord, grant us authority in Thy Spirit to serve You in meeting the needs of others, even when the challenges are disconcerting. Increase our confidence through assurance of our inclusion in the Kingdom of Heaven. Reveal to us more and more of Thy nature and purpose and the thrust of Your Kingdom. Bless our eyes to see You, our ears to hear You, our hearts to know You, our minds to obey You, and our hands to serve others in Your name.

We wince at the story of the Good Samaritan. We are dismayed to remember the times when we crossed to the other side of the street to avoid a direct encounter or responsibility when someone was struggling. We were busy. We were afraid. It was someone else's job. Our plans were too important to be interrupted. It was not convenient to assist. It was risky or costly and we had other plans for our resources. We prayed as we passed by, but we didn't stop to show mercy.

We confess that we have been more concerned to study the scriptures than to live them. We rush anxiously about, tending to our own priorities, and lashing out at anyone who dismisses the value of our busy work. Help us remember that what is needful is always disruptive to the status quo of our lives and plans. Help us to center on You and to choose the good portion of life with You that will never be taken away.

We pray in the name of the One who stops to help us, Amen.

# Luke 11:1-4

*Read carefully and prayerfully.* Reflect on the truth that speaks most clearly to you. Pray your own prayer in response to the Word of the Spirit to you. Offer the following prayer if it helps you express your thoughts to the Lord.

## Prayer of Response

Lord, what a prayer that must have been. When the disciples heard it, they wanted to know how to pray like You. They had heard the prayers in the synagogues. They had heard the prayers in their families and among themselves. They heard something different in Your prayers. They were aware that John's disciples had been taught a prayer form, so they, too, wanted a model, a pattern; but most importantly, they wanted a prayer that works! We do, too.

They wanted to get it right because they wanted results. We do, too. They recognized a difference in Your praying, and it created a longing to enter into prayer in Your manner of communion in the Spirit. Were they surprised by the answer? We are. Your prayer model is brief and consists of only two parts: glory toward God, and simple, basic concerns for ourselves and our relationships. But its simplicity invites us to embrace its potential.

Father, hallowed be Thy name. May Your name be praised through my actions this day, in all my thoughts, words, and prayers. Lord, may Thy Kingdom come, Thy will be done in my life as in the saints of the ages. I bring my soul to bow before You in every choice, decision, and activity. May Your reign be full and complete in all my undertakings. Help me seek only what I need in order to live according to Your purpose. Help me trust You in all things day by day. Forgive my failures to do so. Forgive my striving to do more, be more, and have more. Forgive my pride in multiplicity rather than simplicity.

I come before You in deep and sorrowful contrition for my many, manifold sins and failures. This is a polluted world and I have been soiled by its allurements. Wash me until I am whiter than snow. Cleanse me; purge me from all iniquity so that my prayers may be effective. Help me have compassion on those who have also failed — deliberately, intentionally, callously, willfully — or ignorantly, carelessly, unwittingly. Lord, I know I should release the wounded pride, hurt feelings, and desire for vindication. Even before they confess, repent, or apologize — or don't — I know I must be merciful. You call us to harbor no grudge, nor to plan any revenge.

I understand that I must make the first move toward reconciliation, rather than write them off. I must overcome my shame, disgrace, and embarrassment in order to reach out, and admit my failure. But, I must also overcome my anger from offences against me and open a path for reconciliation with my offenders.

Lord, forgive me for imprisoning others at a distance, for going on as if their lives don't matter. Forgive me for ignoring their value, discounting their worth and denying their potential. I have built barriers beside theirs and the fence has shut me out as well. It is much easier to keep it this way. Help me take up the hard work of dismantling walls and building bridges, intentionally and patiently.

Lead me so I will not fall into temptation. Direct my focus toward the right understandings, right interpretations, and righteous actions that create harmony in community. Lord, teach me to live as You taught us to pray. Amen.

# Luke 11:5-13

*Read carefully and prayerfully.* Reflect on the truth that speaks most clearly to you. Pray your own prayer in response to the Word of the Spirit to you. Offer the following prayer if it helps you express your thoughts to the Lord.

## Prayer of Response

Lord, thank You that we can count on You to give good gifts. If we ask for forgiveness, You will not shun us. If we ask for guidance, You will not misdirect us. If we ask for salvation, You will not condemn us. If we seek Your yearning will, You will reveal it. If we knock on Your door in prayer for others in need, You will answer speedily.

That, perhaps, is the key to the meaning in this story. It is about other-focused and need-based prayer — isn't it? This is not a blanket, free coupon to ask, seek, and knock for things that satisfy our wants and desires. That becomes clear in the promise that the heavenly Father will gladly give the Holy Spirit to those who ask — to those who realize that that is ultimately all we need. When we have the presence of Thy Spirit, we have what we need for responding to the needs around us. The Spirit gives light and life, wisdom and compassion.

Without the Spirit, we have nothing of lasting significance to give our friends. We may share things and ideas of passing value, but only in You do we find the deep answers to pressing need. Forgive us for being empty when our friends need us. You are willing to fill us. We have been reluctant to be filled, because we are reluctant to live precariously by faith. Come, Holy Spirit, come quickly and fill my soul with all Your fullness of love, peace, wisdom, and the power to live selflessly in a greedy world.

Lord, I ask, will You give me the Spirit — even me? Lord, I seek — really seek, because Your Word promises the gift. Lord, I knock — really knock — on the door that opens to faith. And I open — really open — the door of my life to Your loving will and wisdom. Come, Heavenly Dove. Come, Rushing Wind. Come, Spirit of Fire. Fly in. Rush in. Burn within me. Burn the dross away. Fill me with Thy purity. Be Christ in me, the hope of glory. Amen.

# Luke 11:14-36

*Read carefully and prayerfully.* Reflect on the truth that speaks most clearly to you. Pray your own prayer in response to the Word of the Spirit to you. Offer the following prayer if it helps you express your thoughts to the Lord.

## Prayer of Response

Lord, we need to see clearly. We need the light of Your Spirit to illuminate us within and the world without. We need to perceive where You are at work and so join with You. We don't want to be a part of that which disintegrates. We have come to believe that You have brought the Kingdom of God near to us. You have even said that the Kingdom is within us. Your work was the work of God, as if the very finger of God had healed the mute man. One stronger than any evil has come. One with more powerful words than Jonah has come. One wiser than Solomon has come.

When we are with You, Your light shines into our whole being until we can see clearly what is right and what is wrong. We confess that we have been divided in our allegiance. Lord, help us sweep our interior house clean and quickly fill our hearts with unwavering faith. I want to hear the Word of God and to keep it, for in it is hope. In it is love. In it is wisdom. In it is power.

Establish Thy Kingdom in my soul, O Lord. Reign there supreme. Guard my interior palace in peace. I honor Your presence and revere Your name, O Lord God of the Universe and of my life. Amen.

# Luke 11:37-54

*Read carefully and prayerfully.* Reflect on the truth that speaks most clearly to you. Pray your own prayer in response to the Word of the Spirit to you. Offer the following prayer if it helps you express your thoughts to the Lord.

## Prayer of Response

"Teacher, in saying this, You reproach us also." We, too, are full of negative thoughts. We, too, have sat down with a group and sized up the people around us, condemning them in our hearts, exalting ourselves with meticulous manners, and displaying our best wit and nuggets of knowledge. We are Pharisees, neglecting what is important to You: justice, mercy, and kindness toward others. We go to church, sing the hymns and praise songs, give an hour of service and an offering — only to leave in anger, prejudice, and judgment.

We tithe from the material, but not from the heart. We sing Your praises, then seek ours. We are clean on the outside and soiled on the inside. We have desecrated Your temple — the life You have breathed into our soul. We are Your "cup" and we need to be emptied of our worthless musings and plotting. We talk a good game, even witness about You, while all the while denying the full implications of Your truth for our inner and outer lives.

We are innately full of ourselves and deficient in spirit. Lord, cleanse us inside and out. Help us refocus our priorities to love of God and the genuine dedication to righteousness in mind, heart, soul, and body. Help us to refuse false actions of grace and to put away all pretenses. May our lives become containers for Your love and mercy, freely poured out, without reproach, to all. Amen.

# Luke 12:1-34

*Read carefully and prayerfully.* Reflect on the truth that speaks most clearly to you. Pray your own prayer in response to the Word of the Spirit to you. Offer the following prayer if it helps you express your thoughts to the Lord.

## Prayer of Response

Questions come to mind, Lord. Why do we not judge for ourselves what is right? Why do we cover up what should be revealed? Why do we hide what is or should be known? Help us learn the lesson of Judas. What was whispered in the dark is still being viewed and remembered two thousand years later. His shame and disgrace have been revealed for centuries. He thought he knew better than Jesus how life should go. He thought thirty pieces of silver would serve him better than trusting Jesus' way of being in the world.

How easy it is to lose sight of what really matters. How easy to disbelieve that God matters and reigns. Who really believes today that there is judgment and hell? Who believes God watches over every hair and sparrow? Do I? Lord, I'm caught up with the world, in family and cultural matters of judging and dividing. I'm caught up in materialism — in collecting and serving as curator of a cache of possessions — when I know full well that there is only one treasure that will last. Everything we own can be lost in a moment, in the blink of an eye. So it is clear that we need to focus on what will have value when everything else is gone, including our own lives.

Lord, help me to stand out from the crowd and to seek Your Kingdom as my greatest treasure. Help me count everything else as worthless in comparison. Help me live for and by Your divine guidance and reign. Help me no longer toil anxiously, but rather purposefully, with the eyes of my soul always on Your truth, which transcends all earthly knowledge. Change my worldview to Your Kingdom view. Help me believe the value of my life in Your eyes and choose Your wisdom for living it. Lead on, O King Eternal. Amen.

# Luke 12:35-59

*Read carefully and prayerfully.* Reflect on the truth that speaks most clearly to you. Pray your own prayer in response to the Word of the Spirit to you. Offer the following prayer if it helps you express your thoughts to the Lord.

## Prayer of Response

Lord, in every line of the scriptures there is a nugget of wisdom ready to be mined. The answer to the question of countless skeptics is here: "What will happen to those who have never heard of Jesus?" Will God condemn those who never heard his name? Jesus said the one who did not know and did wrong will be treated mercifully and fairly. It follows that the one who did not know and did right will be treated mercifully and fairly. We need to be more concerned about what happens to those who *do* know and yet do not do what the Master wants.

Thank You, O God of Mercy and Grace, that Your judgment is not harsh and punitive, rigid and mean. Lord, clean the scales from our eyes and help us see clearly what the full impact of Your love means. Awaken us to the true reality of life so we can expend our energy for what matters. Help us live in joyous anticipation of Your arrival in every moment. Help us be ready, faithful, wise, and at work on meeting needs — not causing needs.

I have been given much, Lord. Help me give much. Cast the fire of the Spirit upon me, and strengthen me to do what's right when all that has mattered to me may be on the line. Help me to judge the conditions and dangers of the times and to use all the resources of the Spirit to accomplish Your purpose. Help me keep my focus where others lose theirs. Forgive me for relying on what cannot give salvation and on those who have no authority in heaven.

You have asked the question that we must answer: "Why don't you judge for yourselves what is right?" Good question. We fumble for answers. How is it that we can know so much and still make foolish decisions? We can interpret science and history, but overlook the clear indications of things that are wrong in our lives and in the world around us. We get jaded and persuaded, blinded and misguided. We make wrong alliances, accept false precepts, and end up divided from those who matter the most.

We need to hear again the words of Proverbs 3:5: "Trust in the Lord with all your heart and lean not on your own understanding; in all your ways acknowledge him, and he will make your paths straight." It is hard to learn the lesson, but it is the lesson to be learned. We must look to the Lord in all our ways — all our decisions, choices, and undertakings. To rely on our own understanding is to miss the wisdom that God waits to give to those who wait for Him. Our paths will meander in crooked directions until we do.

Lord, I am sobered by these thoughts and turn back to place my faith in You as the One True God and Father of my being. I have being because You *are* Being. I have life because You *are* Life. I have spirit because You *are* Spirit. It is more than enough. You are worthy of all my trust. My cup runneth over. Amen.

# Luke 13:1-9

*Read carefully and prayerfully.* Reflect on the truth that speaks most clearly to you. Pray your own prayer in response to the Word of the Spirit to you. Offer the following prayer if it helps you express your thoughts to the Lord.

## Prayer of Response

Lord, these are troublesome words, spoken in troublesome times, much as we live in today. We can bring our newspapers or display our newscasts about the horrific atrocities, barbaric evils, and intense suffering of the world — lay them alongside Your teachings and it would all correlate. In our day, we, too, long for relief and answers. We're surprised that You gave no direct answer to the specific event of concern. We're even more surprised that You seem to indicate that there is a path that takes us away from such dangers or takes them away from us.

We're mystified and dismayed. We have seen little relief from the constant barrage of evil intent and natural disasters. We must ask: how can our repentance keep towers from falling and rulers from cruelty? Do You mean that such unrest and violence results from not seeking God's will? We understand that repentance is in essence a return to God's will rather than our will. Surely, that is the right path. Whether it changes the world news and our security or not, it would change our personal history for the better.

Choosing God's will would put us in places we would not have chosen, at times we would not have chosen. The fig tree is our paradox. We are planted in this world to produce fruit and we are chronically deficient. Repentance puts us in touch with God's loving purpose and righteous fruit is the outcome. A better life would have to be the result, although history has shown that evil is never fully averted, even for the most righteous of God's followers. But, greater stability is worth choosing Your will rather than ours.

Lord, that's the life I want and the direction I choose. Help me live entirely by Your will, step by step, hour by hour, moment by moment, without fear of the outcome. Amen.

# Luke 13:10-21

*Read carefully and prayerfully.* Reflect on the truth that speaks most clearly to you. Pray your own prayer in response to the Word of the Spirit to you. Offer the following prayer if it helps you express your thoughts to the Lord.

## Prayer of Response

Lord, I get it. The Kingdom of God is not like what happened in the synagogue. It's not like what happens frequently in church. The atmosphere of the Kingdom of God is not toxic. It is not characterized by complaining, criticizing, judging, condemning, and nitpicking. It's about releasing and rejoicing, healing and celebrating. Here is a woman, released from eighteen years of suffering, shoved aside as religious leaders squashed her delight over such magnificent victory over sin, illness, and death. Jesus brought the Kingdom of God to light by forgiving sin, healing illness, and overcoming death. Religious rulers ignored the marvel and condemned the freedom. It happens in church today.

Thank You for revealing that the Kingdom of God is not about rules and regulations, and the Sabbath is not about working or not working. Lord, help us to reorient our views of the Sabbath, to engage in the practice of stepping back to reflect on all Your works, and to join in Your Sabbath rest by mirroring intentional acts of deliverance, rescue, grace, mercy, and unconditional love. Lord, help us in our churches to reflect the Kingdom of God as welcoming and sheltering to all. Help us do the quiet work of faith, loving each person one by one until the whole church is permeated by divine love like yeast in dough — until the whole world is touched by irrepressible love.

Help us make compassion our hallmark rather than our orthodoxy. Maybe that's the mustard seed — compassion. We see in Your life that it is the hallmark of the Kingdom of God. So we need to plant it in our churches, cultivate it to grow, and provide refuge for all. Help us to make church like a joyous circle dance of love that others can't wait to join. Amen.

# Luke 13:22-35

*Read carefully and prayerfully.* Reflect on the truth that speaks most clearly to you. Pray your own prayer in response to the Word of the Spirit to you. Offer the following prayer if it helps you express your thoughts to the Lord.

## Prayer of Response

Lord, thank You for giving us the password to the Kingdom of God: "Blessed is he (and she) who comes in the name of the Lord." The door opens for those who welcome You, the One who came (and comes) in the name of God, and for those who love as He loves. Those who want to be gathered under God's sheltering wings may enter. Those who want to plan and carry out devious and murderous agendas will be barred from the entrance until they drop their wicked intent. Their baggage will not fit through the doorway. They will be left on the outside, holding the deep bags of regret and the anguish of missed opportunity. They are thrust out by their own pride and inflated sense of power and control. We are sobered by the realization that "we" may be "they."

Lord, let us not join in the wailing and gnashing of teeth of those in the depths of despair over missing the entrance. Keep our eyes trained on the entrance and the size of the doorway. Help us lay down all that hinders our entering in through the narrow door to life as You described and designed it. Help us downsize, offload, and leave behind all that will not fit through the door. We don't mind being last. We just don't want to be "out." Gather us, O Lord. Draw us away from the pack of those who become workers of iniquity.

We don't want to forsake the house You offer and we don't want our house to be desolate. Truly we declare, "Blessed is He Who comes in the name of the Lord." Blessed are You, O Christ. Amen.

# Luke 14

*Read carefully and prayerfully.* Reflect on the truth that speaks most clearly to you. Pray your own prayer in response to the Word of the Spirit to you. Offer the following prayer if it helps you express your thoughts to the Lord.

## Prayer of Response

Lord, we are all such mixed bags. We know Pharisees, Sadducees, and Herodians today — by other names. And sad to say, we are often like them and/or among them. We build ideologies and make commitments to current cultural themes and overlook those people in our midst with infirmities or needs. We dismiss their importance, deny their value, ignore their voices, and bypass them. We walk on by, looking the other way. We avoid letting their issues bog us down.

But You always went straight to the one most in need, the one whom others would stifle and shut off. You bypassed those with perceived authority; You denied their self-centric and group-centric importance. You did not allow laws to bind You or to prevent compassionate service. You exalted the poor, the maimed, the blind, and the lame. We hear the call to follow and to live a just life based on the principle of love for all.

While we make excuses, You move on, gathering all who are broken, lonely, grieved, and sick. Lord, wait! I didn't realize what I was doing. Or did I? I recognize that I have placed my allegiance with the wrong ones. Help me turn a deaf ear to even the most cherished relationship and commitment if it distracts or hinders me from truly following You. Help me see, really see, what allegiance to You really requires. I want to renounce the lordship of persons, possessions, and culture that stands in the way of my walk with You.

I want to truly BE Your disciple — "salt that is salty" — living by faith that is faithful, service that is selfless, and love that is genuine. Help me be in the resurrection of the just. Raise up justice in my life day by day. The cost of blind commitment to culture is too great. At any cost, I declare that You alone are Lord, Son of God, The Way, Truth, and Life. And I want to follow in that way — Your way. Amen.

# Luke 15

*Read carefully and prayerfully.* Reflect on the truth that speaks most clearly to you. Pray your own prayer in response to the Word of the Spirit to you. Offer the following prayer if it helps you express your thoughts to the Lord.

## Prayer of Response

Lord, surely there is no passage of scripture more beloved than this one that depicts Your diligent seeking out and rejoicing over one who repents. We see You go after the ones who are lost until they are found. But the passage's layers and depths of meaning appear numerous. We also see the reward of diligently seeking for what we have lost: innocence, purity, righteousness, joy, faith.

We rejoice to see that You receive sinners and eat with them. Thank You that You watch for us and have compassion on us. Thank You for Your embrace and kiss. Thank You that we are never less than Your child, no matter how far we roam. You will never treat us in any way other than as Your beloved child, even when we are not worthy to be called Your child — especially then. Thank You for Your patience as we struggle to accept such unconditional love for others and for ourselves.

Perhaps that was the older son's problem — he had perceived the father as taskmaster rather than loving father. He had distanced himself, though he never left the property. He kept himself on the back porch while the party was going on because he had not yet accepted the father's best gift — love and forgiveness — as his inheritance. Lord, we see how it is possible to be near, yet far; close, but separate. Help us truly believe that we are always with You and that all You are is open to us. Help me find my way fully into Your waiting, longing, loving circle of welcome, O Lord, Our Father in Heaven. Amen.

# Luke 16

*Read carefully and prayerfully.* Reflect on the truth that speaks most clearly to you. Pray your own prayer in response to the Word of the Spirit to you. Offer the following prayer if it helps you express your thoughts to the Lord.

## Prayer of Response

Lord, it is hard to make the transition from the world's view to Your view. Help us see as You see. Help us see the unrighteous ways in which we engage the world and our relationships in it. Help us comprehend what is an abomination to You. Teach us to be shrewd in opposing dishonesty and immorality. Help us see through the sham of what the world approves and what it dismisses. Guide us to use the resources of the world only for good, as faithful stewards of what belongs to another.

Keep us mindful that we did not create ourselves and that we ultimately do not own anything, for at death we hold nothing. How foolish to serve that which is not the ultimate source and end of life. How foolish to justify ourselves in the eyes of some people, while dismissing the value of others. We exalt what we should condemn. We change allegiance; we hurt and offend our friends and family, turn our backs on our commitments, and live in alienation with a false sense of justification.

Keep us mindful that there is no turning back with death. Now is the time to change. You have clearly taught that we need to get our lives right now, before we reach the great chasm of death. We need to notice the people inside and outside our doors and treat them as equals. The rich man depicted in Your parable did not change after death, although he suffered in regret. He still saw Lazarus as less than him, a mere messenger at best. Sobering.

Lord, help me change and enter the Kingdom of God as a faithful steward of this precious opportunity called life.

# Luke 17:1-19

*Read carefully and prayerfully.* Reflect on the truth that speaks most clearly to you. Pray your own prayer in response to the Word of the Spirit to you. Offer the following prayer if it helps you express your thoughts to the Lord.

## Prayer of Response

Jesus, Master, have mercy on us. Your sayings are startling and hard, and our faith is indeed small. I have not wanted to move a tree and plant it in the sea, but I have wanted the courage to admit error, the wisdom to resist subtle temptation, the faith to believe in Your love, and the strength to forgive myself and others. That is a big mountain to be moved.

Help me take heed of myself — really know myself — and what I need to disavow in my life, within and without. Help me to take sin seriously. Help me to reject sin in myself and to warn others when they are entrapped by it or on the verge of stumbling into it. Help me fear nothing so much as responsibility for others falling into sin. Forgive me, Lord, for not barring the door to the temptation that seeps into our lives in the guise of fun, humor, entertainment, recreation, knowledge, and status. Increase our faith, Lord. Help us "plow" and serve without complaint, and with the honest desire to accomplish the good purpose set before us.

Help us take nothing for granted, and to recognize Your help as we go along our way. At the end of the day, may we reflect, without regret or resentment, on all that has been accomplished. May we reflect with satisfaction on commitments fulfilled. And let us go to our chambers at night in peace and thanksgiving for the opportunities, blessings, and gifts of the day.

Like the leper who turned back to express his thankfulness for his healing, may we make it our life's habit to turn back to You in praise and gratitude for the experiences and lessons of each day — and with utmost faith to greet the sun of tomorrow in the joyous anticipation of another day of living in Your grace. Amen.

# Luke 17:20-37

*Read carefully and prayerfully.* Reflect on the truth that speaks most clearly to you. Pray your own prayer in response to the Word of the Spirit to you. Offer the following prayer if it helps you express your thoughts to the Lord.

## Prayer of Response

Lord, it is so surprising to recognize that we look for You and Your Kingdom in all the wrong places. Your Kingdom is not where it can be observed with human vision. It is hidden well by our own assumptions. There are no tangible signs to look for. I could not have readily discerned it within the circle of Your followers; for we, like they, all fail so much. But it is found where You are, where You are revered, believed, trusted, and followed through the ups and downs — even among Your fallible followers. We encounter it in our church family, misshapen as that family may be.

Thank You for these words of clarification that help us seek Your quiet presence rather than a spectacular manifestation. Forgive us for seeking wonders, or not seeking anything of You at all, while we thrash headlong through the affairs of our lives, heedless of Your nearness. Help us to stop our incessant activity and to go within, where You meet the seeking soul.

Help us heed Your warning that we can attain all our goals in life, yet miss You — the true essence of life. Help us abandon self-focused goals and worldly promises in order to go with You and not look back. Lord, lead me; call me; remind me that You are within as much as without, near as much as beyond. Light up the sky of my life with the radiance of Your truth. Gather me where Your people come together to form the Body of Christ. Help me renounce the useless pursuits and empty dreams that fill and waste our days in the world.

In the midst of my clamoring to succeed at and accomplish what I have been misguided into valuing, I have had a glimpse of Your true nature and purpose. Help me to quietly and quickly turn away from all that distracts so that I may become caught up with You only. I stand before Your unpredictable and uncontrollable power and am dismayed. I am unworthy and overwhelmed by the jeopardy in which I have lived. Help me let go and let Your life be all that matters.

Come, Lord Jesus. Amen.

# Luke 18

*Read carefully and prayerfully.* Reflect on the truth that speaks most clearly to you. Pray your own prayer in response to the Word of the Spirit to you. Offer the following prayer if it helps you express your thoughts to the Lord.

## Prayer of Response

Lord, I come to receive my spiritual sight — to be made whole and well. But I confess, I want it for my comfort more than for Your glory. But I do want to change and to be made right with You. So, I come to pray and not lose heart, to cry out day and night for Your guidance, healing, and forgiveness. Like the Publican I moan, "Lord God, be merciful to me a sinner." I take comfort in Your assurance that God does not respond to us reluctantly, but speedily.

There is not much that encourages faith in the world today. In the exaltation of self, we have lost our childlike wonder. In our rational pursuit of empirical evidence, we have put up barriers to having faith in possibilities beyond our understanding and experience. When the ruler asked the fundamental question of life, You invited him to get off the roller coaster and get his balance again. You challenged him to let go of all hindrances to life with God.

Help me take a detached view of all that I claim to know and delight to own. Help me relate to all I treasure as You did in the walk toward Jerusalem, ready to lose all in order to fulfill all God's love for us. It is truly hard for me to imagine literally selling all I have in order to give to the poor and to be rendered poor myself, dependent on the generosity of others and Your supply. It really does seem impossible and, to my rational mind, impractical. So I cry out with blind Bartimaeus, "Jesus, Son of David, have mercy on me." I am full of my own desires and knowledge, and blind to Yours. How should I answer the question, "What do you want me to do for you?"

Lord, I want the courage to seek nothing but the Kingdom of God. I want the determination to deny myself any thought, word, relationship, deed, or possession that hinders me from eternal life. Lord, let me receive my spiritual sight and know the truth that will set me free from what binds me to all I have.

Jesus, Son of David, have mercy on me. Amen.

# Luke 19

*Read carefully and prayerfully.* Reflect on the truth that speaks most clearly to you. Pray your own prayer in response to the Word of the Spirit to you. Offer the following prayer if it helps you express your thoughts to the Lord.

## Prayer of Response

O, Lord, would that even today we embraced the things that make for peace — and that all the people of the world knew the ways of peace. Would that all the people knew that You have come to us as God would come. We have seen divine love in action, calling a short, despised tax collector to dinner. We have seen the love of God reach past all barriers to the children of Abraham — children of faith who amend their lives to match Yours.

Help us to heed the warning of the parable and to be active in increasing the value of Your name and gifts in the world. Though You are able by Your own power to multiply all that is, we are blessed to partner with You in increasing faith, hope, and love in the world. Lord, keep us focused on what is most important: reaching out to seek and save the lost, those struggling without faith in You.

Train our vision to notice those who yearn and try to know You and improve their lives. Help us call out to them, to welcome them, to minister to them, to encourage and equip them to walk in Your ways. Teach us to be faithful in the little things that we don't think matter or make much difference. Cleanse us from our visions of grandeur and acclaim which blind us to the truly fruitful and fulfilling pursuits in life. Lord, whatever You want of us, we want to provide. Well, that is what we know we should say; but our hearts are deceptive. Help us to become willing to want what You want. Let us not be counted among those who do not want You to reign over them. Drive out the attitudes that rob faith and joy from our lives and the world.

Blessed is He who comes to us as God — to be believed and obeyed. We are astonished at such a simple entrance into the life of blessedness. It is so doable, yet we procrastinate. Truly, blessed art Thou, O Lord our God, God in the flesh, Creator, Sustainer, Redeemer, Savior. To You and You alone belong all power and glory and honor for all time and eternity. May we hang upon Your every word, listen daily to Your teachings, and together make a house of prayer for the world — a temple and issuing place for Your Spirit. Amen.

# Luke 20

*Read carefully and prayerfully.* Reflect on the truth that speaks most clearly to you. Pray your own prayer in response to the Word of the Spirit to you. Offer the following prayer if it helps you express your thoughts to the Lord.

## Prayer of Response

Lord, in which group am I? Would I be among the hungry souls hanging on every word as You teach in the temple? Or, would I join the legalists, marveling at and yet threatened by Your answers, demanding to know Your credentials of authority? It occurs to me that hungry souls seek authenticity above authority.

The soul knows Truth for its capacity to bring balance, stability, wisdom, peace, and hope. Help us know the Truth that will set us free from the paralysis of analysis that binds us in a rational paradigm. Your words are Spirit and Life. Your parables are living and active, palpable with reality. You created and planted a vineyard for mankind to cultivate and You send forth servants to help in the process. More often than not, they are maligned, opposed, and treated as worthless — then sent away empty-handed.

People are laid off, forced into retirement on low pensions, beaten down with discouragement, and no one takes heed of the atrocities. It is justified as necessary for the greater good of the corporation or institution — a "good" that enriches some at the expense of those who don't measure up to the cultural, social, or productive requirements. People do all these things while being fully aware that Your words truly teach the way of God — a different way, a compassionate way. Forgive us for our duplicity and help us forgive others.

Forgive us for knowing truth and remaining silent, for rendering unto Caesar what is God's, and unto God what is Caesar's. We are conflicted, and guilty of allowing wrong to reign. We, too, have pretended to be sincere in order to further our own security or prosperity, to hide our insecurity and poverty of spirit. We, too, raise smoke screens of speculation to obscure truth and blind ourselves to Your reality.

Give us the long vision, Lord, to see past the truncated philosophies of the world to the eternal truth that endures. Help us let go of the short-lived honors of the world so that we may take hold of the resurrection life. May we grow and live into the life You offer us as children of resurrection hope — joining the angels in the glorious state of the Beloved of God.

What a lofty prospect for humans! We have so much more to claim than mere earthly glamour and status. Help us so live as to be deemed worthy of attaining a future life among those who live to You and not to the world.

Though we don't like to consider it, it is possible to live in danger of Your condemnation, which is a far greater loss than worldly goals; and it is a totally avoidable condemnation, one that we choose by the decisions we make. Lord, I turn to sit at Your feet as a learner and bow before You on the cornerstone of Your authority over life and death.

May I live differently, reverently, purposefully, committed to Your way of love. Amen.

# Luke 21

*Read carefully and prayerfully.* Reflect on the truth that speaks most clearly to you. Pray your own prayer in response to the Word of the Spirit to you. Offer the following prayer if it helps you express your thoughts to the Lord.

## Prayer of Response

Lord, this raises sobering questions for each of us: Will I be among those who are maligned, accused, and condemned by family, friends, and religious or political authorities? Do I live for You so faithfully as to draw persecution? Do I have to? Is it a prerequisite for the Kingdom? I don't want to miss the Kingdom. It is clear that troubling times such as You have predicted begin in the seedbeds of complacency and tolerance, but also in fear and carelessness. I don't want to be lost in complacency or ambivalence.

There is a cumulative effect in our world even now so that we can easily imagine it becoming an avalanche of evil like You have depicted. Let us not be lulled into sleepy faith when we need to be alert. More importantly, help us to not cringe in fear when we should warn others that we are headed into a tsunami of religious and political upheaval. While I do not desire such horrors, and will flee if faced with them, I would rather be among the faithful who are targeted than among the perpetrators or tacit supporters of ideologies that lead to such calamity.

These are already confusing times, with many cultural issues that defy logic and challenge faith. Within the same household, family, church, and/ or workplaces, people may vote for different candidates and support various conflicting issues. In fact, we all seem to live with contradictory convictions that fuel inner and outer turmoil.

So, Lord, let me live today as if the predicted apocalyptic age were our current context. Help me live each day as if this is the only time I have to bear testimony for my faith — for the gospel. Like the poor widow who put all she had in the temple treasury to honor God, help me put all I have into Your service. Remind me that the goal is not to be liked, not to live a life of ease; the goal is to honor You regardless of the consequences.

I want to endure by faith. I want to trust You with my life and to be faithful, even when all whom I love may stand against what I stand for. Even now, tumult is the result of speaking out, and my natural inclination is to shrink back from conflict. Lord, strengthen me, so I will not miss the opportunity to stand before the Son of Man among those who gain life by releasing what we can't hold on to anyway.

Keep me alert to opportunities in which Your Spirit will fill me with the wisdom to speak of what is eternally true. Help me know the difference between what matters with You and what is of eternal irrelevance. I'm looking up, Lord, for the fulfillment of Your promised redemption. I need You to guide me so that I will not be led astray by authoritative voices, nor intimidated by earthly power and influence. Draw near, O Christ, to sustain Your servants and protect us for Your Name's Sake. Amen.

# Luke 22:1-38

*Read carefully and prayerfully.* Reflect on the truth that speaks most clearly to you. Pray your own prayer in response to the Word of the Spirit to you. Offer the following prayer if it helps you express your thoughts to the Lord.

## Prayer of Response

Lord, we live betwixt and between. We live in Your Kingdom and in the world. We live as citizens of the world and transgressors in Your Kingdom, for we deny You and fail to uphold what we know to be true. We seek prestige in leadership rather than humility in selfless service. We are more inclined to follow the voices of worldly authority than Your voice of invitation. Pray for us, O Lord, that our faith fails not. Thank You for reckoning Yourself with us — unruly and untrustworthy as we are. Help us live honorably and honestly in the overlap between Your Kingdom and the world, letting go of all that hinders our progress with You. Strengthen us to manage our affairs in the world as witnesses and ambassadors of a higher realm.

We earnestly desire communion with You. We open the upper room of our hearts to You. Come and feast with us. May each participation in the Lord's Supper be blessed by Your presence in the Spirit. Break thou the Bread of Life and nourish us with strengthened faith. Pour for us the cup of the New Covenant in Your blood and ratify the constitution of Grace for us in Your Kingdom. Thank You for Your body given for us.

Help us use our bodies for You and for everlasting good. Forgive our betrayals and help us turn again to follow You, and to strengthen one another in faith. We praise You for Your great salvation, for all that You have prepared for us, down to the most infinitesimal details. It is enough. Amen.

# Luke 22:39-46

*Read carefully and prayerfully.* Reflect on the truth that speaks most clearly to you. Pray your own prayer in response to the Word of the Spirit to you. Offer the following prayer if it helps you express your thoughts to the Lord.

## Prayer of Response

Lord, over and over again You and the angels spoke the comforting words, "Do not fear." Is that what the angel said to You in the garden? When fear and dread were pouring out from Your very veins in sweat and blood, did the angel stand by You and say, "Do not be afraid"?

We are more often encouraged with words such as, "Buck up! Keep your chin up!" Such words are like telling a fire not to burn. They have no effect on human fear, which can grip, engulf, and entangle us in a heartbeat. New experiences of dread reverberate back down to every fear we have ever known and we can become deeply shaken. We need to hear the words over and over: "Do not fear." It is so much easier to fear than to trust. So, thank You that those three words were spoken so often in the pages of scripture.

This scene encourages us to understand that You know what it's like to lie awake in the dark, consumed with dread. Certainly, You know what it's like to pray, "*IF* it is Your will, let this cup pass from me." Sometimes we find it hard to trust that God can, or will, help us. You prayed our prayer as You entered fully into our fear. You understand our "Ifs." And You instructed the disciples: "Pray that you will not to be put to the test" — or not fall into temptation (as expressed in the NIV). Thank You for giving us permission to come to You with our fears and our weaknesses. You don't expect us to make it on our own, to pull ourselves up by our own bootstraps.

We take heart in how Your humanity and divinity swirled in and out with human passion, pain and fear, as well as divine love, compassion, and trust in the Father. As we grow in You and You in us, that swirling is in process; we live in the tension between fear and trust, humanity and Spirit. To fear is human. To trust is divine. It is Your life in us that enables us to trust. Lord, give me more of Your life. Fill me down to the deep recesses where my fears hang out. I hear Your challenge to awaken from my sleep of dread and to "Get up and pray" — so that I will not fall into temptation or be put to the test with little faith to withstand it.

Lord, I come to You in order to confront my fear with prayer rather than running in circles. I pray to live in confidence that the angels who strengthened You are nearby to strengthen us, if we will but give ourselves to honestly facing our fears before You. Thank You that You do not expect us to be fearless — only to face our fears in faith. Amen and Amen.

# Luke 22:47-71

*Read carefully and prayerfully.* Reflect on the truth that speaks most clearly to you. Pray your own prayer in response to the Word of the Spirit to you. Offer the following prayer if it helps you express your thoughts to the Lord.

## Prayer of Response

Lord, we marvel at the power of language, especially in Your words. Living by faith is about listening, really listening, to Your language. It is about praying, really praying, in Your dialect. This passage is about the power and righteousness of God at work, in contrast with the power and ill-directed authority of man. We arm militias to settle scores while You declare two swords "enough" against a mob. We start crusades to conquer the godless while You heal the wounded. It is hard for us to think Your thoughts, talk Your language, and walk in Your steps.

To survive in this world, we are completely dependent on You and upon a change of heart and mind. It is beyond our understanding to own a sword and not to use it. We want to prepare. But why buy a sword when You will tell us to put it back in its sheath? The disciples were not trained to fight—only to pray, preach, teach, and care for others. It is so counter-intuitive to the ways of the world.

You call us to be transparent even as the world plays a game with opaque rules of denial and cover-up. That is our temptation: self-preservation. It seems so logical. Peter was bent on being of support to You, on getting farther than the others in standing by You. He thought he was playing smart, pretending, covering up, protecting himself, and inadvertently doing just what You said he would do — denying he ever knew You. Peter's denial and Judas' betrayal stand through the ages as stark reminders that faith can be readily overturned. It is troubling to read that Satan entered Judas and Judas sold out. His story is disturbing because we know how tenuously we hold faith ourselves.

O Lord, turn and fix Your gaze deeply into our eyes. Help us understand the ways in which we are enmeshed in worldly practices that are in contradiction to the way of Spirit and Truth. Lord, lead us so we will not fall into temptation. Open our eyes. Awaken us from our sorrowful slumber of soul and help us face reality with the faith that we follow the One seated at the right hand of God, who has come to us and lived among us as one with no guile.

Truly You are God in the flesh, for only God could be in the world as one with pure, selfless motives. The world hates Your ways, though, as much as ever. The world hates all those who will not retaliate and dominate, or conform to the standards of those who do. It is hard, Lord, to be maligned and reviled, mocked and mistreated. But, You know that. You shared our pain and understand why we waiver and vacillate between Your call and the world's. It is easy to pray, "Father, if thou art willing, remove this cup of suffering from me;" but it is hard to pray, "nevertheless, not my will but thine be done."

It is hard to let Your way of love be done — Thy way of honesty to be done — Thy way of praying to be done. The Spirit is willing but the flesh is weak. Truly, Lord, may Thy way of righteousness be done in my life and in the lives of all who long to see God and to know God. I believe Yours is the right and true way of Life and I want to live in it always. Amen.

# Luke 23

*Read carefully and prayerfully.*

Reflect on the truth that speaks most clearly to you. Pray your own prayer in response to the Word of the Spirit to you. Offer the following prayer if it helps you express your thoughts to the Lord.

## Prayer of Response

Lord, my attention goes to the centurion, a Roman soldier who had led and witnessed many executions. But there was something different in this death. He had never seen a convulsion of earth and sun — the very ground of being convulsing in chorus with the human pangs of suffering. He had never witnessed a man who seemed to some extent to be in charge, committing His Spirit to a God whom He called Father. He normally witnessed a convulsion of soul and body in torment, often the angry cries of anguish penetrating the eerie silence, damning God and the executioners while vultures awaited their pick.

Jesus had forgiven his enemies from the cross, praying for God to forgive them in their ignorance. The authorities hardly seemed ignorant. Those astute religious leaders knew all the ins and outs of government, the laws of the land, and their religious heritage. Yet, they did not understand the laws of God's Kingdom. Their minds were blocked by their system of doctrine, power, and greed. But for one of the criminals crucified with Him, it was clear that a travesty had occurred: an innocent man who truly knew God was dying at the hands of unjust men and beside unjust men. And He gave love rather than hatred to His tormenters.

The insightful sinner on the cross wanted to be received into a Kingdom where such power of love reigns; and You welcomed him — the sinner who praised Your righteousness. Just as You had made no comment to Pilate, You made no comment to the one who mocked You. Help me learn to speak only welcoming, helpful words, and to be silent in response to criticism. I see that defensiveness is the way of the world and not of faith. Faith is steadfast in love and righteousness and is a powerful influence. Defensiveness is self-defeating.

It is sobering to read of how urgently and feverishly the religious leaders worked to condemn You. Though it was clear to outsiders that You were innocent and not deserving of death, to the Pharisees, because of Your acts of gathering wheat and healing on the Sabbath, You deserved stoning. They believed that it was their duty to uphold the commands that they believed

had been given to Moses by God. They mixed cultural practices of decep-
tiveness with religious legalism and bits of distorted truth to confuse the
people and to force their will through the Roman legal system. Cleanse me
of similar double-mindedness.

It was true that You taught throughout Judea — and opened blind eyes,
restored deaf ears, healed diseased and deformed bodies — demonstrating
the power of God. That was brushed aside as irrelevant, and the profane
crowds were manipulated into preferring that an insurrectionist and mur-
derer be released. Barabbas was freed while You were mocked, beaten,
tormented, and crucified. Pilate could not withstand the demands of the
crowd; he released the one deserving death and condemned the one who
deserved no death. Forgive me when I give in to the loudest voices rather
than the still small voice of truth.

I correlate this account of Your sufferings and death with the statement
of Paul: "For the wages of sin is death, but the free gift of God is eternal life
in Christ Jesus our Lord" (Romans 6:23). Like Barabbas and the thief on
the cross — and the religious authorities — we could be justly accused of
moral and ethical failure. We deserve our "earnings" for sin. Yet, the pure
Son of God died; the One who could not die gave up his life. This was not
merely another tale in human history of the execution of a just man and
innocent victim. This is the One who laid the foundations of the world and
holds the keys to life and death. It is a mystery to be contemplated soberly,
for much of scripture attests that the execution was because our sins were
laid on Him as Isaiah predicted:

> *Surely he took up our infirmities and carried our sorrows;*
> *yet we considered him stricken by God, smitten by him and*
> *afflicted. But he was pierced for our transgressions, he was*
> *crushed for our iniquities; the punishment that brought us*
> *peace was upon him, and by his wounds we are healed. We*
> *all, like sheep, have gone astray; each of us has turned to his*
> *own way and the Lord has laid on him the iniquity of us all.*
> (Isaiah 53:4-6 NIV)

The mystery rings out across the ages in the words of Jesus: "Father, forgive them for they know not what they do." The whole of scripture points
to this remarkable, tragic scene and says God was at work. In a mysterious
way, God saw all our sins, failures, and misunderstandings represented. As
Paul said, the Lord triumphed over our sin, "having canceled the bond

which stood against us with its legal demands; this he set aside, nailing it to the cross" (Colossians 2:14 NIV).

We praise You, O God, that the curse of eternal death was averted for all who call upon You for righteousness. We know that, had we been there, we could have betrayed like Judas, denied like Peter, lied like the Pharisees, shouted with the crowds in our confusion, executed with the soldiers, quaked like Pilate under pressure — and walked free like Barabbas.

One who deserved no death received it, and those who had earned death through sin were welcomed into Paradise. Amazing. Grace. Amazing Grace. Father, into Your hands I commit my spirit. You have opened Paradise to all, and I join the thief on the cross in praying, "remember me when You come into Your Kingdom." I receive Your forgiveness gladly and seek Your counsel and guidance that I might walk and talk in the ways of Your Kingdom now. Amen.

# Luke 24

*Read carefully and prayerfully.* Reflect on the truth that speaks most clearly to you. Pray your own prayer in response to the Word of the Spirit to you. Offer the following prayer if it helps you express your thoughts to the Lord.

## Prayer of Response

Lord, open our eyes that we might see wonderful truths revealing Your ways. Help our eyes focus and recognize You. May all we see around us expand our understanding of essential truth. Forgive us for seeking living truth among those who are dead in faith, who depend only on rational, scientifically proven theories, and who consider biblical stories to be "idle tales."

Help us remember Your words and the power of inner light which they ignite. Strengthen our faith in the Good News concerning You, revealed in Jesus of Nazareth, who was condemned for our sins and who redeemed us from eternal death. That is a hard word for some to hear today. It does not connect with "Enlightenment" thinking. It is strange that the awakening of reason is called enlightenment, when it sometimes dims the light of the gospel for many. We forget that Jesus said he came to those who need healing, not for those who do not.

For those whose lives are broken, their sense of worth diminished, burdened with a sense of guilt and shame, only atonement makes sense. But it is the atonement of a loving God, rather than an angry, demanding Judge. It is the atonement of John 3:16: "For God so loved the world that he gave his only Son, that whoever believes in him should not perish but have eternal life."

That is the only gospel that sets the sin-sick souls free. Help our churches keep that door of liberty open for those who are heartsick beneath their burdens of guilt over missed opportunities and poor choices in life.

Interpret for us all things concerning Yourself. Help us to overcome our disbelief, with joy and understanding, by coming to see the scriptures as a portal through which we may enter in order to know You. Help us read differently, with an awareness of Your nearness. Stay with us, for it is far into the night of ignorance and disbelief. We need Your presence. Break bread with us and bless us with awareness of all truth concerning Your great offer of salvation. Burn indelible marks of spiritual reality within our hearts. Relieve us of our troubled, questioning hearts by clear indications of Your resurrection power. Clothe us with power from on high, the promise of the Holy Spirit, the gift of the Father.

Lead us to witness about all that You have taught us, so that others may repent of their unbelief and share the grace of forgiveness and reconciliation. May we always be found blessing God with great joy as the One who has come to us in Christ. May we always be found praising Christ Jesus, who lived and died and lives again, who reigns in Your Kingdom of love at the right hand of God the Father Almighty, who loves like a Tender Mother. Amen.

## Note

[2]James McGranahan and Daniel W. Whittle, *There Shall Be Showers of Blessing* (Public Domain, 1883).

# *Praying Through John*

## John 1

*Read carefully and prayerfully.* Reflect on the truth that speaks most clearly to you. Pray your own prayer in response to the Word of the Spirit to you. Offer the following prayer if it helps you express your thoughts to the Lord.

### Prayer of Response

Lord, this is such an astounding chapter. It stands so many things on end. We are left gaping in astonishment. The One who declared, "Let there be light" embodied that light-giving power on earth (Genesis 1:3). The Word that expressed God's will in the dawn of creation — expressed it in flesh and blood. The One who had no beginning brought a new beginning for people who welcome Him as He welcomed us.

This is a chapter of welcome. The Son of God beckons and welcomes. The Law that came through Moses was fulfilled and surpassed by a superior Law of Grace. The Law that judges, condemns, binds, excludes, and kills was overtaken by Grace and Truth, which forgives, heals, and welcomes. The Word of Creation, the Word of Law and Prophecy, entered the human realm and made God fully known beyond stone, temples, and rites. The Light of Redemption shone into the world in a blazing glory that cannot be surpassed or dimmed.

Now anyone can become a Child of God and commune with the Almighty God of Heaven and Earth, for the Son of God has come to take away the sins of the world that blocked that communion. Take them away from my soul, Lord — as far as the east is from the west, beyond the reaches of all eternity. Free me from the burden of feeling vaguely unworthy and release me to feel clearly forgiven.

We are assured that all who receive Jesus and believe in Him as Son of God, Lamb of God, God of God, receive the blessing to become a Child of God. Lord, I know You as all of that and more. You are the One who hears my prayer in this moment, and this searching soul is a lost child seeking my Eternal Father and my Eternal Home. Thank You that You came and unceasingly come with words of invitation: "Come and See. . . Follow Me." Lord, I come. Lord, I follow. Let me see Your glory, the glory of Grace and Truth, shine into my life and overcome the darkness of shame and blame.

Your life is our Bridge, our Hope, our New Life. It would be amazing to see with spiritual insight and to behold the heavens opened and the angels serving God and man in the new way You have opened. I long to see that in eternity; but, most of all, I need to know its effects in my life in the here and now. I pour out my heart and ask You to baptize me in Your Spirit in the here and now. Lord, I want to prepare the way in my heart for You. Please take away the sin of the world that I have accepted in my life. Wash me that I may be clean — whiter than snow. I fall before You with wonder at the power of Your grace and truth. I want to bask in the marvel of Your love until I am able to live without guile and can bear witness that You are the Lamb of God who takes away the sin of the world.

Glory to the One and Only, full of Grace and Truth, who came from the Father into our troubled existence so that we could find our True Life. Amen.

# John 2

*Read carefully and prayerfully.* Reflect on the truth that speaks most clearly to you. Pray your own prayer in response to the Word of the Spirit to you. Offer the following prayer if it helps you express your thoughts to the Lord.

## Prayer of Response

Lord, when You come to Your temple in my soul, what would You overturn and throw away? What is unfitting today? What should be driven away? May zeal for Your house consume me. Let me not rest until Your Spirit can rest in me as a fit dwelling place of peace and righteousness.

Thank You for the extravagance of Your love and mercy symbolized by 180 gallons of wine rather than a few cups. Help me change my focus and purpose to be aligned with Yours. I want to do whatever You say. I want the water of my life changed into the new wine of an eternally meaningful life. I want my life to count, to bring joy into the lives of those in darkness, and to be the best I can be.

Lord, You know all that is in me which prevents that outcome, for You know what is in the dark recesses of all minds and hearts. Please, Lord, drag it out and take it away. Raise up new life in me, life that honors God and glorifies Your name. I believe in You, in the scriptures about You, and in the Word which You have expressed through words and actions of love and grace.

I believe You are the Christ, the Light of the World, and the Hope of my life. Amen.

# John 3

*Read carefully and prayerfully.* Reflect on the truth that speaks most clearly to you. Pray your own prayer in response to the Word of the Spirit to you. Offer the following prayer if it helps you express your thoughts to the Lord.

## Prayer of Response

Father, we see that Your love for Your only Son, Jesus, is the foundation of our hope. You have given all things into His hands, including our eternal salvation. He comes from above and is above all. Lord, we set our seal to this — that God is true and that the One he sent utters the True Words of the One True God. May His glory increase while our self-aggrandizing decreases. O Lord, let there be less and less of my self-importance and more and more of Your omnipotent glory.

We begin to glimpse Your glory when we see Jesus. When we are born anew through faith in Him, we see with the radiance of the Light of the World. You reveal what we have hidden and stumbled over. Lord Jesus, You have revealed God's amazing love to us. You have descended from heaven that we might ascend to heaven. You have brought God to us and us to God through new birth. Yet, we often feel so out of touch and out of step. Help us let go of "flesh" and take hold of "spirit."

May the wind of Your Spirit blow away the debris and reveal what really matters to us and to You. Help us receive Your testimony and believe that You, O God, have so loved the world that You have sent Your only Son, Jesus, to release us from real and "felt" condemnation. We rejoice to be "saved" by grace, through faith. As the Israelites looked to the brass serpent on a pole as confirmation that God would heal their snakebites, so we look to the cross as confirmation that we are healed of our sin "bites" (Numbers 21:9 NIV). We rejoice in the marvelous exchange of our sin for Your righteousness. Thank You for taking our overflowing cup of failure and replacing it with Your overflowing cup of grace.

Though it is improbable and irrational to the secular mindset, it is irrefutable to our true soul. Nothing else brings peace to a sin-sick, needy soul. Only atonement can make us believe that we can be made whole, for our sense of estrangement and alienation requires assurance of the certain defeat of our burdened conscience. Baptize me in its reality and truth until I am finally and completely free and clean.

Love to You, O God, Father, Son and Holy Spirit. Amen.

# John 4

*Read carefully and prayerfully.* Reflect on the truth that speaks most clearly to you. Pray your own prayer in response to the Word of the Spirit to you. Offer the following prayer if it helps you express your thoughts to the Lord.

## Prayer of Response

Lord, the story of the centurion and his dying son reveals faith formation in levels. It reminds me of electronic games in which an action can take the player through a door or to a higher level. The centurion believed at "Level 1" when You said, "Your son will live." But he entered a higher level when he received word from his servants that his son was healed at the very time Jesus said the words. At that level, he entered the door of convincing faith that influenced his entire household to believe. The woman at the well moved quickly through the levels to convince her entire community to believe. She moved from cautious skepticism to full-blown faith in action.

We marvel at Your gift of faith. It flows like water, blows like wind, reaching every corner and filling every hole of our lives. Faith, in the living power of God at work in the Spirit, is like living water that never fails and always refreshes, springing up and running over eternally. Lord, give me this living water that I may not be constantly seeking refreshment from temporary sources. Quench my thirst with the joy of faith so that I will never thirst again. I want this gift of God welling up in me to higher and higher levels, overflowing to touch the lives of others, influencing at least a portion of the world for good, and flowing powerfully into eternal life.

Help me refuse to get caught up in useless religious controversies and wrangling, but to stay instead in the stream of believing grace. Help me stay focused on the Father and to worship from the heart in faith that expresses itself in action, in spirit, and in truth, for I know that Messiah has come! Christ has come! I believe, not only because of others' testimony, but because You have spoken to me, called me by name.

Lord Jesus, I rejoice to call You by name, and I pledge to follow You into the fields that are ripe for harvest. I am ready, Lord, to enter into the labor of gathering fruit with You, for I know that You are the Savior of the world, my Savior and Lord, the Lord of the Harvest. But the spirit is willing and the flesh is weak. Stay near me and strengthen me in conviction and commitment. I know and am convinced that You who speaks to me through Word and Spirit are "He" — the only "He" that matters now. Amen.

# John 5

*Read carefully and prayerfully.* Reflect on the truth that speaks most clearly to you. Pray your own prayer in response to the Word of the Spirit to you. Offer the following prayer if it helps you express your thoughts to the Lord.

## Prayer of Response

Lord, these are heavy words, saturated with potent meaning. I am dismayed, for I recognize how endangered we all are. We are entangled in a world system, not unlike the paralyzed man who had put his faith in an empty system for healing. He had waited for thirty-eight years to be healed, through the "health system" of his day, believing he was dependent on someone being there to help him at the right moment.

Lord, help me know the difference between popular, cultural faith and living, active faith. We can lie for thirty-eight years in a pseudo-religious pursuit, blaming and making excuses for our problems and bad luck, expecting and experiencing only more miserable waiting. The question I hear is, "Do you want to be healed?" I hear inherent in it, "Do you really want the responsibility of living by active faith? Have you become so resigned to your paralysis of faith that you have lost sight of God's care and love? Has He faded behind myths and doubts?"

The message is clear to all of us, "Look up, the water of life has been stirred!" Jesus has come — Son of Man and Son of God, with "healing in his wings" (Malachi 4:2 KJV). He hasn't come to put any of us into the pool of superstition or futility, but to give us the strength and courage to obey Him and to walk a new life. I hear, "Rise, take up your pallet and walk" — walk into a new future. Walk into God's love and Grace. Walk by humble, grateful obedience to God and not by prideful confidence in human intention that results in distracted inattention.

I hear Your Word that we need to know You and follow You, no matter who or what may seek to deter us, for in You we encounter God's merciful authority and His everlasting love. In Him is the light of life. In Him is resurrection. He and He alone can raise us up to eternal life. We cannot be too dead in sin or despair for Jesus to lift us. The words of a popular hymn say it clearly: "Turn your eyes upon Jesus. Look full in His wonderful face and the things of this world will grow strangely dim in the light of His glory and grace."[3]

Lord, forgive me for looking and not seeing, for hearing and not trusting, for believing and not acting, for living and not loving, for learning and not obeying, for running and not following, for waiting and not expecting. Come again, Lord Jesus, to my pool of shame, disgrace, sorrow, and despair. Enlighten my understanding, strengthen my resolve, and enable me to live as a credible witness to Your power, wisdom, and love. Amen.

# John 6:1-14

*Read carefully and prayerfully.* Reflect on the truth that speaks most clearly to you. Pray your own prayer in response to the Word of the Spirit to you. Offer the following prayer if it helps you express your thoughts to the Lord.

## Prayer of Response

Father God who feeds us, we are amazed — not just at the signs Jesus performed, but that Jesus Himself is the Bread You have given to feed the world. It is beyond remarkable for more than 5,000 people to be fed from five barley loaves and two fish. But it is more astounding to understand that there was something even more profound going on than satisfying the physical hunger of a multitude. You are feeding the world.

Just as You fed the Israelites manna in the wilderness and just as You fed the 5,000 by the Sea of Galilee, You continue to feed us what will nourish us forever. In the giving of Jesus, You have fed us His very life — Your life. Through his body, You demonstrated Your abiding love. You fed us love. Through Your incarnate blood, as the Lamb of God, You have covered our sin. Through Your acceptance of the cross, we are accepted just as we are. Through grace, You have cleansed us. You satisfied us with forgiveness. You fed us hope, assurance, joy, and more and more blessings besides. You have fed us food that abides forever. It cannot be gathered up into baskets, but it can be shared.

Lord, we understand our responsibility to let none of all that You have done be lost or wasted. As John gathered up all the stories that reveal Jesus as the Bread of Life, we must gather up and share all that has been given to sustain us. Jesus does something more than feed us with what we can see, touch, hold, taste, and swallow. He gives us hope that abides forever. He gives us eternal food. He gives us what the world cannot give. He gives Eternal Life. He gives us His very own Spirit.

Lord, though there is much we do not understand, we know there is no one else to whom we can turn and receive the life of heaven. We believe You are the Holy One of God. You and You alone have the words of eternal life. The words that You have spoken are full of Spirit and Life and we receive them gladly. We open our souls to receive and share Your very life. May every morsel of food and drop of beverage remind us that You feed us. We live because of You and we live forever through You — through Your love, mercy, power, and grace. Amen.

# John 6:15-21

*Read carefully and prayerfully.* Reflect on the truth that speaks most clearly to you. Pray your own prayer in response to the Word of the Spirit to you. Offer the following prayer if it helps you express your thoughts to the Lord.

## Prayer of Response

Lord, we cannot leave this chapter without pausing to contemplate what happened on the Sea of Galilee in the dark of night. Alone in the boat, bewildered because You had not returned, needing to get home, uneasy in their ponderings, they struggled to make sense of all they had seen and heard. Perhaps feeling abandoned, they forced their boat toward home against a strong wind and high seas. Their fear and confusion engulfed them when they saw Your form walking on the choppy sea. They were glad to hear Your voice, and they were eager to receive You into their boat.

Lord, we have no problem imagining that scene. We are frightened today, battling headwinds that threaten to sink us, unsure of where You are as we grope in the darkness of our troubled souls. There are strong currents, high waves, and blustery winds in the surrounding culture that threaten our well-being and buffet us with anxiety. We are eager to receive You into our boat. Lord, come to us, too. Let us hear Your voice calling out to us, "It is I. Have no fear." We are straining to hear that reassurance. We are straining to see You through the dark, foreboding clouds of despair that surround us.

Lord, please enter into the boat with us and help us steer a safe course home. While people clamor to figure You out by reason, help us to be content to know by faith that You have come to us and all is well because You are here. We have not trusted an illusion. We have grasped the true reality. Amen and Amen.

# John 6:22-34

*Read carefully and prayerfully.* Reflect on the truth that speaks most clearly to you. Pray your own prayer in response to the Word of the Spirit to you. Offer the following prayer if it helps you express your thoughts to the Lord.

## Prayer of Response

Wow! What a power-packed passage. This needs to steep in my heart for a while. Sight and logic can take us only so far. The people knew enough to know there was no way Jesus could have crossed the lake, but he was not there with them. So curiosity drove them to explore farther and to cross the lake themselves. Jesus did not answer their verbalized question of how he got there — but he answered the question in their hearts. They were operating on the tangible level; He was on the spiritual level of what really matters. He pointed beyond the signs that enamored them by satisfying their human needs, to that which will satisfy them forever. Am I on that level yet, Lord? Raise me up, Lord, I pray.

Help me live above the desire for notoriety such as they displayed in asking, "What must we do to be doing the works of God?" They wanted to be able to feed 5,000 and to walk on water. They wanted to see and eat manna such as their forefathers had. You answered by leading them to the right question. They should have asked, "What is the food You give me that will endure to eternal life? How do I receive that food?"

Lord, I want that food, the true bread from heaven. I want You, Lord Jesus, who has come down from heaven and gives life to the world. I believe that You are the answer to all our needs and longings. Come, Lord Jesus, fill our hungry souls to overflowing. Let me place my hand in Yours and partner with You in feeding the multitudes the Bread of Life. Amen.

# John 6:35-51

*Read carefully and prayerfully.* Reflect on the truth that speaks most clearly to you. Pray your own prayer in response to the Word of the Spirit to you. Offer the following prayer if it helps you express your thoughts to the Lord.

## Prayer of Response

Lord, thank You for the invitation — to come and not hunger, to believe and not thirst. There is movement, of person and life, necessary for having our deepest hunger and thirst satisfied. We cannot stay in the same place. We must move our whole being toward You, O Christ. Thank You for drawing us to Your table, Lord.

But we have to partake. It is possible to come to You and still not partake of all You provide. We must also believe. The people of that day wanted more signs, more proof, more evidence before partaking. We do, too. You require that we get past our arguments and enter the door marked "Faith." I want to enter that door and lose nothing of all that God has given for eternal life. I want to be raised up at the last day with You, O Christ. When that hope is what I crave, I know that my real hunger and thirst will be quenched.

We can see that doing the will of God satisfied the hunger of Jesus, and it will satisfy ours. Stir my hunger and thirst, Lord; and feed me, quench me, till I want no more. Amen.

# John 6:52-71

*Read carefully and prayerfully.* Reflect on the truth that speaks most clearly to you. Pray your own prayer in response to the Word of the Spirit to you. Offer the following prayer if it helps you express your thoughts to the Lord.

## Prayer of Response

Jarring! That is what Jesus was. The Jews were God-interested, God-fearing people who held His name in high respect and sought to earn His favor by carrying out religious laws. But Jesus jarred them. He rattled them out of their complacency by working unexplained and unmatched miracles of divine power, and then teaching lessons that flew in the face of their carefully restricted culture.

Jesus said He came down from heaven, but they knew his human origins. They knew his folks — they could call them by name. It blew their minds for him to claim to be the Bread of Life. He claimed we must eat the Bread of Life because the Bread of Life is His flesh that He gives for the life of the world. And the shock reverberated still further when he said we must drink his blood. Selah. I need to pause and think about that, too.

This is a hard saying. It sounds gross, like cannibalism. It sounded like the practice of pagans, which Israelites had been taught to condemn — and which is anathema to us, as well. Even the disciples were horrified. We are taken aback, too. But, for those who trusted Him and were willing to look beyond the words to the truth they represented, a new reality emerged. It is a relief to know that the promise is of the Spirit. Receiving the Spirit of Christ, being nourished by His Spirit — that is what gives life. We can't just know his body was crucified. We can't just know his blood was shed. We can't just have the rational facts. We have to internalize the reality of what was happening in Jesus — of what He was doing for us, and of what He wants to accomplish in us.

Lord, I join with Peter. I don't want to leave, even though I don't fully understand. I want to be fed and nourished. No one else but You has the words of eternal life that nourish my soul. I believe and know that You are the Holy One of God. Choose me, Lord. Feed me, Lord, with Your righteous life so that I may live forever.

Thank You for Your amazing gift in flesh and blood that gives life to all those who come to the table with believing hearts. Amen and Amen.

# John 7

*Read carefully and prayerfully.* Reflect on the truth that speaks most clearly to you. Pray your own prayer in response to the Word of the Spirit to you. Offer the following prayer if it helps you express your thoughts to the Lord.

## Prayer of Response

Belief. It's all about belief. It's only about belief. Lord, why is that so hard for us? We ponder. We rationalize. We see, hear, and doubt, like Your brothers. We murmur with trusted people, but we are reticent to talk openly about our deepest thoughts of You. We analyze and rationalize, deny the obvious in favor of a philosophy, putting human ideas before spiritual realities. We question and debate, weighing opinions and the facts at hand. We divide into camps around our conclusions. We expend tremendous mental and emotional energy, to no avail.

All we have to do is believe. It is clear; we have to accept You, O Lord, by faith, which is in itself a gift of Your grace. It is a new way of living beyond the scope of our earthly limitations. It connects us with the realities of Spirit in Your way of life. Lord, help us who believe plunge by faith into the Living Water of Your Spirit. Help us to drink deeply, swim freely, and lose all our weighty concerns and arguments. Teach us, O Lord. Help us accept Your divine authority and live in Your will — Your yearning.

Remind me daily that "no one ever spoke the way this man does." You and You Alone have the key to abundant and everlasting life. Amen.

# John 8

*Read carefully and prayerfully.* Reflect on the truth that speaks most clearly to you. Pray your own prayer in response to the Word of the Spirit to you. Offer the following prayer if it helps you express your thoughts to the Lord.

## Prayer of Response

Lord, we are faced with this over and over. This chapter raises the two crucial questions: (1) Do we really believe? (2) How can we *keep* Your Word? For You have said repeatedly that we must do both. To continue in Your Word is to believe You are in God and God is in You. To continue in Your Word turns on the light so that we can see and know Truth and be free to speak and act by Truth. Lord, help us keep Your Word, for You have promised that those who do will never see death.

Yet, everyone dies, the righteous and unrighteous. The body gives way to disease, injury, and aging; but the soul that believes never gives way, never sees an end to life. It continues with You. Thank You for Your Word of hope so we will not walk in darkness. Yea, though we walk through the valley of the shadow of death, we will fear no evil. The Light of the world is with us to dispel the darkness, so we see no frightful, dreadful specter of death. We see only an open way, a bright passage, and an expansive welcome.

To believe Your Word is to recognize Your personal assurance that You have released us from our prisons of doubt, fear, guilt, and shame. We stand before You, justly deserving no mercy. Yet You bend down to our level and You write softly in our dirt that we are forgiven. We hear the stones of judgment drop at Your feet and the dreadful sounds of condemning voices fade away as You say, "Neither do I condemn You."

Lord, there is no greater deterrent to sin than those words. We want to hear those words. We want to keep those words, Your Words, tucked close to our hearts — treasured, cherished, believed in with no uncertainties. We do believe that You are as God is and God is as You are. We are amazed at Your startling Word — that God judges no one. He judges actions. He forgives persons. Lord, we are free indeed. We have seen and heard the truth that transcends all barriers and frees us from all our guilt and shame.

Hallelujah to the Great I Am! Hallelujah, what a Savior! Amen.

# John 9

*Read carefully and prayerfully.* Reflect on the truth that speaks most clearly to you. Pray your own prayer in response to the Word of the Spirit to you. Offer the following prayer if it helps you express your thoughts to the Lord.

## Prayer of Response

Lord, I hesitate to ask what the Pharisees asked, but I need to know. I am embarrassed to ask their question, but here it is — am I blind, too? Have I closed my eyes to the brightness of Your truth? Where I do not see, help me to see. I know that I have blind spots, for sure. I also know that You are the Light of the world. You embodied on earth all the goodness, truth, life, and power of creation and redemption — every attribute that enlightens our minds, hearts, and souls.

Lord, we come to the pool of Siloam with the clay packs You have made for our eyes. As we wash in the cool, refreshing, cleansing Living Water of Your Grace, may we come up seeing and knowing You. May we come up believing and following You. May we come up ready to make Your name great among all who recognize they are blind and need to see, all who are sick and need to be well, all who realize that what they know is not adequate. We come in humility and honesty, with our empty cups to be filled with new understanding and purpose.

I believe that You work the works of God. I believe that You have brought merciful judgment into the world — judgment as discernment and understanding — judgment as revelation of light and darkness, truth and error. Help me learn the lesson You taught the disciples: that I do not need to spin my wheels trying to figure out all the cause and effect questions, such as those related to suffering. We need to focus on bringing glory to God through compassionate works of God in our lives.

Open our eyes to the ways we can reveal God's love in our midst, through the light of Christ shining in our lives. Amen.

# John 10

*Read carefully and prayerfully.* Reflect on the truth that speaks most clearly to you. Pray your own prayer in response to the Word of the Spirit to you. Offer the following prayer if it helps you express your thoughts to the Lord.

## Prayer of Response

O Lord, You are my Shepherd, the Good Shepherd who leads me beside still waters and makes it possible for me to lie down in green pastures. You are the one who leads me in paths of righteousness, spreads a table before me in the presence of my enemies, anoints my head with oil, and fills my cup to overflowing. You are our Good Shepherd who lays down His Life for the sheep. I shall not want — I shall not lack. I shall not be lost and forlorn without help in my life, for You are with me.

You are in God and God is in You, to keep and to guard, to call and to guide, to comfort and to save. You nourish me. You redeem me. You lay down Your life and take it up again — to share it with all the sheep in all Your pastures. Yea, though I walk through the valley of the shadow of death, I need have no fear, for You are with me, to strengthen and comfort me, to guide and deliver me, to correct and gather me.

All the circumstances of life become tools in Your hand for instructing me and shaping me according to Your image. You fill me with good things from heaven's table. Your Word is my food. Though surrounded by enemies who seek to steal, kill, and destroy, I dwell secure and confident, anointed by Your grace, mercy, and love. Nothing and no one can snatch me out of Your hand.

Surely goodness and mercy shall follow me all the days of my life and I shall dwell in the house of the Lord forever — not because I have earned eternal blessing, but because You have loved each sheep and given Your life in atonement and redemption. I am Yours. We all are Yours. We have been bought for a price: the precious blood of the Lamb of God, always and only Savior and Lord, who was slain from the foundation of the world (Revelation 13:8 NIV).

I hear Your voice. I hear my name spoken in Your voice. I follow, because I long for abundant life rather than meager earthly existence amidst baubles and bubbles of meaningless pleasures. I want to be in Your fold and to heed Your voice, to go where You go and do what You do.

Lead on, O Good Shepherd. Amen.

# John 11

*Read carefully and prayerfully.* Reflect on the truth that speaks most clearly to you. Pray your own prayer in response to the Word of the Spirit to you. Offer the following prayer if it helps you express your thoughts to the Lord.

## Prayer of Response

Thank You, Lord, for Your tears. Thank You for revealing that You are deeply moved by our human sorrows. It is so hard to accept illness and death. We don't want it. We want You to come and prevent it or take it away — overcome it. So we are comforted to know that You grieve at our loss. But we are like Mary and Martha. We would not have understood why You delayed. You loved Lazarus and his sisters, knew Lazarus was dying, and yet *waited* to go to him. We don't understand why we pray for our deepest concerns and sometimes still have to stand beside a grave and return, year after year, with a fresh batch of flowers.

Show us how to deal with illness and death for the glory of God. Like Mary and Martha, we believe that You can prevent or heal our diseases and injuries that have no human remedy. Help us see illness as a means to glorify God. We do believe that You are the Resurrection and the Life Everlasting, and that those who believe in You do not end in death, but in life with You forever. We believe You are the Christ, the Son of God who walks in immortal light. Help us cease stumbling in the darkness of fear in the face of illness and death. Help us walk in the light with You.

Help us see through our human pain and sorrow to the reality that transcends it. Remove the stone that blocks our understanding. Unbind us from our fears and help us go forth in faith to bring glory to You in life, even through illness and death. May nothing prevent or distract us from faithful witness. Thank You that You always hear us and answer us according to the high and holy purpose of heaven.

Lord, call my name and help me come out of my tomb of fear and regret. Give me the faith to accept Your response to my need, whether immediate or delayed, as Your highest purpose. Amen.

# John 12

*Read carefully and prayerfully.* Reflect on the truth that speaks most clearly to you. Pray your own prayer in response to the Word of the Spirit to you. Offer the following prayer if it helps you express your thoughts to the Lord.

## Prayer of Response

Lord, turn on the light a little brighter. Our eyes have grown dim. The darkness has crept in and overshadows us and our world. We need to see, really see. We need to see Jesus, again, clearly. We need to listen, really listen, to His Word, for they are God's words. Help us fully comprehend that these are words of the Living God for us to hear, really hear. We need to follow what we hear and watch where the words lead — where Jesus walked, where his actions enlightened the people of his day and on down through the centuries. His ways are God's ways. We need to watch, really watch.

Lord, if we comprehend fully, we realize that we need to serve You and Your purpose, abandoning our concerns and fears of losing face, status, and security. We need to break open our treasured alabaster jars of anointing oil — those acts of love that should be poured out with abandon to bless others and to glorify You, O God. We need to take off our coats and lay them in the mud for You as You join the path of suffering with every person in need. We need to wash Your feet with our tears as we recall the times we missed You in the faces and suffering of those who journey alone, without help or hope in the world.

May the light of Your righteousness blind us to the differences in people and allow us to overcome the darkness of prejudice that shuns and excludes. May the grain of wheat in our life be planted deep, deep enough for us to grow and produce seeds of Your life in the world — the world that thumbs its nose at Your reality and sovereignty. May we keep our lives for eternity by loving You and Your way more than our own self-centered way. Help us remember that losing what we cannot hold for eternity is gaining all that matters with You. Encourage us to step down into the role of Your servant in order to step up into the realm of Your reign.

Help us seek not so much to be saved as to save; not so much to be served as to serve; not so much to be loved as to love; not so much to gain as to give; not so much to be great as to be true.

Father, glorify Thy name in us. Amen.

# John 13

*Read carefully and prayerfully.* Reflect on the truth that speaks most clearly to you. Pray your own prayer in response to the Word of the Spirit to you. Offer the following prayer if it helps you express your thoughts to the Lord.

## Prayer of Response

Lord, it is so hard in today's world to know when we are denying and when we are not. We are as clueless as Peter and often deny some aspect of Your ways. We need a rooster that crows each time we deny You in order to alert us and help us retrain ourselves to think, speak, and act in ways that honor You. To attune our thoughts more closely to Your truth, we need a warning that will be triggered when we sidestep important issues out of apathy or fear of losing face or place.

Lord, we want to draw so close to You that we can discern when the morsel of denial has been passed to us. We need to understand clearly how deceptive our own thoughts can be. Wash our heads, hands, and feet, as we are not yet clean all over. We do want to fully partake of Your life and to freely serve those to whom You send us. Lord, here are our hands, our towels, our washbasins. Where do we start?

I think of the Good Samaritan who started with the first person in need that he came across (Luke 10:30-37 NIV). Lift up our eyes to see them today, Lord, and let us not pass them by. Whether it is for someone close to us or for a stranger, help us do as You did. Help us gird our minds to serve humbly, not thinking of anyone as being lower or higher than ourselves, but as all carrying the seed of Your life within them. Show us those who need to be welcomed and affirmed, received and validated. Keep us mindful of the watchword and central thrust You declared: to love one another as You have loved us.

Help us disavow all rationalizations and excuses that cause us to lose our focus. When the world repudiates intentional acts of kindness or creates a hostile environment for goodness, keep us mindful that our love for one another is the light of witness that glorifies You — as Father, Son and Holy Spirit.

We get it! This one thing we *must* do: love all who are in community with You. It is the least and the most that we are to do: love one another. And we are to love all those who have not yet entered into community with You, for You send Your rain and Your sunshine upon all. And *then*, we will be strong enough, together, to love all into the fellowship of the love of God and neighbor.

Help us know most assuredly that we must master the "one another" love for fellow believers. It is the foundation for loving the world to the glory of God. Help us, O Lord, to that end. Amen.

# John 14

*Read carefully and prayerfully.* Reflect on the truth that speaks most clearly to you. Pray your own prayer in response to the Word of the Spirit to you. Offer the following prayer if it helps you express your thoughts to the Lord.

## Prayer of Response

When we turn the page to this chapter, we walk into the arms of God. Twice we hear, "Let not your hearts be troubled." In a crazy world like this, telling us not to be troubled is like telling a fire not to burn. But You draw us close and say, "Believe me. Stop, look, listen. Look at my works; listen to my words. Believe that I am in God and God is in me. Believe — because I have great plans for you and I have shown you the best way for your life. I have given you a path to follow and a counselor to guide you — a counselor who knows all truth — even my very Spirit. I have not and will not leave you desolate. I have come to you — to live with you and within you. Cling to me in faith and love and you will dwell in peace with me and you will know the Father's love."

Lord, we hear! We see! We come! We gasp at the wonder of it all and grasp the key of love that opens our present and our future in You. We know that we barely fathom the depth of Your love — a love so amazing and so true that the world does not readily comprehend it. "Love so amazing, so divine, demands my soul, my life, my all."[4] So, it is not about right doctrine. It is not about knowing or earning anything. It is about receiving and giving love. That's the way. That's the truth. That is the life. That is the standard by which we measure our thoughts, our words, and our actions — the standard of Your all-encompassing, inexhaustible love. That is peace.

Lord, I hear Your call, "Rise, let us go hence." Yes, Lord, let us go where You have prepared for us to go — into the Father's arms of love and out into our up-close world with hearts, hands, and words full of love. We hear an overarching call from You: "Come, let us all love the Father." From the Father, we receive all that we need. We receive welcome. There is a place with God — prepared and ready — and the welcome mat is out. We see it awaiting our footprint. You have shown the way that will get us there — the way of bold, confident, determined faith and love.

Your words and Your works show us the way and the truth and the life to which You call us. Your words have lifted our hope to seek more than we can fully understand — to reach beyond the scope of reason to trust in

Your Spirit. Then we will set our focus on what can be given in Your name and for Your glory. When we learn to listen for Your Spirit within, we see the work You do more clearly and we follow. In love to You we turn, Amen.

# John 15

*Read carefully and prayerfully.* Reflect on the truth that speaks most clearly to you. Pray your own prayer in response to the Word of the Spirit to you. Offer the following prayer if it helps you express your thoughts to the Lord.

## Prayer of Response

Lord, I cherish my place in the vine. Please don't take me away from You. Prune me, but don't discard me; for apart from You, I have nothing, am nothing, and can be nothing of true value. Apart from You, I wither and become useless, devoid of dynamic life.

Thank You that I have been made clean by Your Word. I am refreshed and renewed in hope and ready to obey the will of the Vine, to grow where Your life leads and to put all my energy toward bearing Your fruit. Abide in me and I in You. Like photosynthesis in a leaf, with organelles and mitochondria working incessantly to produce the plant's energy, may Your Spirit work in me to produce the energy of Your life in my words and actions.

I come to the scriptures to find the entry into the life to which You call me, a life marked by right prayer, glory for our Heavenly Father, and the fruit of love that grows from the Spirit of love. Then I can obey Your commands, though the abiding itself is obeying. It is listening, not just for Your recorded words in scripture, but for the ongoing direction of Your Spirit. I know that I must look to You as the author and authority of my life and respond to the nudges of Your Spirit, not as options for my will's consideration, but as commands of Your divine, pure will — with the overarching command being love.

You love, so I must love and can love. Master, I am Your creation — Your servant first and yet "friend" by Your grace. In Your inexhaustible love, I hear Your warning: to love You and be loved by You will bring hatred from the world as I no longer conform to its will. So, yes, Lord, send Your counselor to bear witness in me to Your reality — to strengthen, comfort, sustain, and guide me. Help me remain with You to the end, no matter what threatens to undo our union and communion. Thank You that nothing can undo that union and communion unless I give way to it.

Strengthen me and hold me in the Vine. Amen and Amen.

# John 16

*Read carefully and prayerfully.* Reflect on the truth that speaks most clearly to you. Pray your own prayer in response to the Word of the Spirit to you. Offer the following if it helps you express your thoughts to the Lord.

## Prayer of Response

Thank You, Lord, that You do not want us to fall away. Thank You for all You said to keep us from falling away. Thank You for all You did to keep us from falling away. Thank You for the gift of a Counselor, Your very Spirit, to keep us from falling away. Falling away is a terrible precipice to avoid and we need all the help we can get.

Thank You for the gift of conviction — about sin, righteousness, and judgment. It is hard for our generation to hear words about sin, righteousness, and judgment. Strengthen us against the rushing torrent of unbelief and denial. The world around us is like a vortex pool of irreverent doubt, swirling faster and deeper into intellectual agnosticism. May Your Spirit keep us from being sucked under its power.

Keep us focused on Your righteousness, which transcended death and left an empty tomb in its place. Keep us mindful and grateful that the ruler of this world is judged — and not us. We are forgiven, cleansed, remade in Your image. It is indeed to our advantage that You went away — through atoning death to the Father — that we might go to the Father in union with You. Thank You for pulling back the veil and exposing reality — for helping us see that it is possible to think we are right in our service to God, even when we are absolutely wrong. We welcome Your Spirit to guide us into all the truth, based on Your authority, glorifying You, and teaching us.

Thank You for this rich treasure which fills us with joy in the midst of sorrow. Thank You that we are not alone, that You have not left us as orphans. You have come to us and will always come to us. Our sorrow is turned to joy as we commune with the Father in Your name, Lord Jesus. You have taken us to Yourself like a cherished bride to a beloved bridegroom. So we pray in union with You, and the Father sees and hears us in union with You. We no longer pray as waifs, but as beloved children.

Lord Jesus, we are grateful that we do not have to wait behind a veil, hoping You will pray for us. You pray with us and in us. And the Father loves us as the Father loves You. Therein is our joy, our peace, our wonder, our Beginning and our End. We are of good cheer. You have overcome the world in us. Thanks be to God for His Unspeakable Gift. Amen.

# John 17

*Read carefully and prayerfully.* Reflect on the truth that speaks most clearly to you. Pray your own prayer in response to the Word of the Spirit to you. Offer the following prayer if it helps you express your thoughts to the Lord.

## Prayer of Response

Lord, I get it. We simply must consent to love. It is the way to know You, follow You, and glorify You; it is the only way. It is the way of union with You in the Father. It is the only way. Through love, we enter into the glory that You share in the Father. When love permeates us, we provide a hospitable environment in which the Spirit of Christ can thrive and interact in the world. So, come Lord Jesus. Have power over my flesh and give me eternal life through knowing God — truly knowing the One True God.

Manifest Thy name, Thy power, and Thy glory to me clearly through Thy Word and Thy works. Take my blinders off and help me see. Lord, I do know in truth that You are One with God and that all that is of God is in Thee, and all that belongs to God belongs to Thee. What a glorious reality: I belong to You. I am Thine, O Lord, by Grace and by choice. I have believed, and I do now believe — in God and in You, His Son, Jesus Christ, whom He has sent as the Savior of the world. I want You to be glorified in my life. Guard me, keep me from the evil one, sanctify me in truth, and lead me into fulfillment in Your Joy.

As You consecrated Yourself as a sacrifice for sin, strengthen me in consecration as a living testimony to Your Truth through life and death. I want to be in communion with those who know You, unified in holy purpose in order to manifest Thy name in the world. Lord, Your church in the world is fragmented. In fact, the world has so permeated the church that Your presence is barely discernible to outsiders. May our oneness with You transcend the differences among believers, so that the world may know that You have come and do now live among us. Keep us mindful that we are "sent." It is not about us, or our goals. It is about YOU. And it is about *them* — the ones You came to save — the ones to whom we are sent.

When we know ourselves to be embraced in Your love, we can let go of self and selfish interests. Convince us that we are cared for and that others need that same comfort. We humbly stand amazed in assurance that You are in us and that we are in You, alive forever in communion with all those who have believed before us. May this awareness grow among believers throughout the world and unite us as one Body — Your Body — living, moving, and having "being" together in holy love, for Your glory.

Thy Kingdom come. Thy will be done. Amen.

# John 18

*Read carefully and prayerfully.* Reflect on the truth that speaks most clearly to you. Pray your own prayer in response to the Word of the Spirit to you. Offer the following prayer if it helps you express your thoughts to the Lord.

## Prayer of Response

Lord, we hear the pathos of it all. The secret garden where You and the disciples had often found sweet respite and communion — that holy oasis — was desecrated under the clang of weapons and flash of fiery torches. Peace was shattered and terror gripped Your followers. Betrayal had a face — a very familiar face; and Your first concern was to protect Your followers and to argue for their release. You were the one in charge.

The perpetrators of evil could not stand before You — the *I AM* of God. They drew back. They fell to the ground. You could have escaped. You could have overcome them. Instead, You offered Yourself in exchange for the release of Your disciples. Peter could have fought for You, and did, in a brief defensive strike; the others would have joined in, but You had set Your face toward the cross — to drink the cup of suffering for humanity. You blocked their interference. Your ways are not like our ways, for sure.

For all who have eyes to see and ears to hear, You bore witness to the truth: that Your Kingdom is not of this world. That means there is another "world," one with as much significance, and more, than this one. There is a "sphere" where You reign with ultimate authority over our petty power struggles and pitiful attempts to control destiny. Peter thought he was being clever, covering, hiding, lying — so that he could perhaps yet save the day and be the zealous hero he so wanted to be. But all he was doing was denying reality — resisting Your way of deliverance.

While Peter was denying, Barabbas was being set free. The disciples went free. We are all set free because You were not. Though we, too, have done our share of denying or dismissing the rich truth of the gospel, we also are set free. Though we may go through the gut-wrenching repentance of Peter when we recognize our failure to stand up for the truth, we are set free. Thank You for Your marvelous grace.

Help us to attune our hearts to your voice, ever calling us toward freedom and righteousness. Teach us Thy ways, O Lord. Set us free from ours. Amen and Amen.

# John 19

*Read carefully and prayerfully.* Reflect on the truth that speaks most clearly to you. Pray way own prayer in response to the Word of the Spirit to you. Offer the following prayer if it helps you express way thoughts to the Lord.

## Prayer of Response

Lord, silence seems to be the best response to this passage — this record of the world's greatest travesty and heaven's greatest victory. We are stopped in our tracks when we review this scenario in our imaginations. With heaven's goals accomplished and scripture fulfilled in Jesus' loud call, "It is finished," we marvel at all that has been accomplished; and we wonder where we would have fit in the scene. Would we have reacted differently than the chief priests and religious officers who were repulsed by the sight of Jesus after the scourging — torn, bruised and bloodied, wearing a crown of thorns and mocked, a purple robe hanging limply and pitifully over his devastated frame?

We know that we are not more righteous than past generations. From the appearance of His visage, would we, too, have been convinced that this man was no messiah, no son of God, but merely a charlatan at best? Would we have dismissed the wonders as being done by some demonic means? Would we have accepted Pilate's view and seen Jesus as only another man, unique for sure, but just a man — a pawn in a never-ending round of political maneuvers? This man puzzled Pilate, but he wasn't convinced of either his innocence or his divinity enough to overcome his own fear of losing earthly power or position.

Pilate's declaration, "Behold the man," was replete with irony, as Jesus was truly "THE" man who had riveted the countryside and city streets and had drawn a following described as a "multitude." We are amazed that the multitudes could be so easily diverted by their religious leaders; and yet it happens rather often now, too. It sits like lead in our minds to know that religious leaders could instigate such a horrible miscarriage of justice. It sobers us because we know it still happens. It is sobering to see how they had the crowds whipped into a frenzy, shouting "Crucify him," while Pilate fueled the evil fire still more by proclaiming "Behold your King." Would we have mocked? Would we have called for crucifixion? Sadly — the answer is "probably." In fact, the real answer is that we have, and do, when we are reticent to speak up for Christ or to live for Him.

We can identify with Pilate, in that he didn't plan this. The situation was thrust upon him. The passion of others had set the stage on which he stood; but he had chosen to be on that world's stage, defending what was expedient more than what was right. He did it all the time. Do we? Jesus' passion to honor God and to love all people had threatened the status quo among the Jewish leaders. Their passionate fear of losing more ground to Rome thrust them into a political juggernaut. We get ourselves into jams because of our strongly held goals, too.

Fear won. Extremism won. Self-preservation won. Or, so it appeared — until their awful deed was consummated. Then we are faced with a story that can't be explained away, and an exact fulfillment of Psalm 22. We are touched that Jesus, who was silent under unjust condemnation, spoke out from the anguished position on the cross of Roman execution to arrange for his mother's care and for his beloved disciple's comfort. Like those who saw and reported, we are left speechless, wondering at the meaning of blood and water gushing from His pierced side. Whatever it means, true life was poured out. True love rolled forth like a gentle river.

Would we have joined the two who stepped forward to anoint and bury Him? Then they went home. The crucifixion was finished. What was there left to do but to go home? The "man" was dead. The "King of the Jews" was buried. But the fulfillment of God's plan was more complete than friends or foes could know. That is still the case. His Work is unseen but steady and certain. His Plan unfolds into glory, moment by moment.

Lord, help us look on this scene and accept the sobering conviction that You were no ordinary man and no ordinary king. Lord, we open our hearts and minds to understand more. We confess that we display some of the same characteristics as the unbelieving rulers, crowd, and followers of that day. And like the crowds, we watch but don't get too close. Like the disciples, we retreat to safer ground. Like the soldiers, we look for ways to benefit, if only with part of a garment.

Lord, help me step forward like John and Mary and stay close to You. Help me come out of hiding, like Joseph and Nicodemus, and attend to Your body. Lord, I anoint You in my heart and lay You to rest there. Rise again, Lord. Fulfill Your purpose in my life. Lamb of God, I place Your blood on the doorposts of my heart. Save me, deliver me and my household from wrong directions, wrong beliefs, and wrong choices.

I look upon the one who was pierced and I marvel. Lord, remember me and bring me into Your Kingdom. Amen.

# John 20

*Read carefully and prayerfully.* Reflect on the truth that speaks most clearly to you. Pray your own prayer in response to the Word of the Spirit to you. Offer the following prayer if it helps you express your thoughts to the Lord.

## Prayer of Response

Blessed Lord, it is indeed a miracle when anyone believes. I'll never forget my reaction when I first shared the gospel with someone who believed after considering the truth. When I asked if she wanted to receive Jesus into her heart and she said "yes," I blurted out, "You will?" It's humorous now, but it was in that moment that I really knew the gospel is for real. I had known it in my mind, in my convictions, for my personal need; but then I knew it in power — not mine, but the Spirit's.

Here, though, we come to an audacious, improbable story — of angels in white who roll away stones, terrify soldiers, attend to a resurrected body, guard empty grave cloths, and comfort astonished followers. We face the story of a crucified man, transformed and living in a body, appearing first in the garden and then in locked quarters, bearing the wounds of the crucifixion, all the while bearing the evidence of a life transitioning to heaven. We marvel at this account of the Divine Holy Spirit given to men simply by breathing on them. Here we have the power to forgive sins transmitted to mortals. But the greatest mystery is the union with God given to men and women.

It takes my breath away! If You, O Lord Jesus, have ascended to Your Father and *my* Father, we are One! If You have ascended to Your God and *my* God, we are united in a reality stronger than death and stronger than life as we know it. This is a story that I believe because it is the only truth that makes sense. Outlandish as it is to scientifically conditioned minds, it is the only story that opens a path of peace. It is the only story that opens a path of forgiveness and that taps into the best strengths of mankind. It is a God story and it is a human story.

Roll away the stone from our minds and help us look into the empty tomb and see You. Come to me at the entrance of my tomb of despair and fear. Call me by name and assure me that You are with me and that I am with You, unified in the Spirit for all time. Nothing can sever our union, because You have brought it about. Breathe on me and all Your people — blow on us the gift of Thy Holy Spirit and empower us with wisdom to go where You send, to forgive what You forgive, and to declare truth where wrong exists.

We rejoice to have life through faith in the Name, the Person, and the Power that is in You, O Christ Jesus, Son of God. Amen and Amen.

# John 21

*Read carefully and prayerfully.* Reflect on the truth that speaks most clearly to you. Pray your own prayer in response to the Word of the Spirit to you. Offer the following prayer if it helps you express your thoughts to the Lord.

## Prayer of Response

Lord, like Peter, we don't know how to get started in following You. We more often settle back into the routine of our culture, never forgetting what we have learned, but not clear about what to do about it either. We know "It is the Lord." We know we have met You. We know You as the Divine Man. We know the biblical record is true and not fact or fable. WE *know.* But we don't know how to live outside our ruts. We are the masters of our fate within our spheres of accomplishment, until You help us see that it's not really working for us all that well anymore. It is just comfortable, familiar. We're just stuck, afraid to embark upon a path that we have never known.

So, we look around. We wonder whether others are following, and how they're following, and what their results are. We're waiting for some clear sign that this way is going to work out well for us. That's our problem — or my problem. It's a focus problem. I'm concerned about *me* and the outcome for *me.* Help me to set my focus on You, to listen to You, to follow You, and to shepherd Your sheep, Your people, the young and the old.

Lord, show me which side of the boat to fish from in order to gather in Your people. Teach me how to feed them and guard them and guide them into the fullness of Your love. No matter what, Lord, here I am. Whether it's many people, or a few, or one, Lord — here I am to follow You. Here I am to stay focused. Here I am to feed Your lambs, tend and feed Your sheep. Here I am, walking with You and never walking alone. Here I am, fishing with You and never fishing in vain again. Here I am, fed by You and never hungry again.

Lead on, O Good Shepherd. Amen.

## Notes

[3]Helen H. Lemmel, *Turn Your Eyes Upon Jesus* (Public Domain, 1922).
[4]Isaac Watts, *When I Survey the Wondrous Cross* (Public Domain, 1707).

CPSIA information can be obtained at www.ICGtesting.com
Printed in the USA
BVOW06s0445190615

404506BV00003B/4/P